Top 25 locator map
(continues on inside
back cover)

Cork City
WITHDRAWN
FROM STOCK

CityPack

San Francisco

Top 25

MICK SINCLAIR

If you have any comments or
suggestions for this guide you
can contact the editor at
Citypack@the AA.com

AA Publishing
Find out more about AA Publishing and the wide range
of travel publications and services the AA provide by
visiting our website at *www.theAA.com/bookshop*

About This Book

KEY TO SYMBOLS

 Map reference to the accompanying fold-out map, and Top 25 locator map

⊠ Address

☎ Telephone number

⊙ Opening/closing times

🍽 Restaurant or café on premises or nearby

Ⓢ Nearest subway station

Ⓡ Nearest railroad station

Ⓑ Nearest bus route

🚢 Nearest riverboat or ferry stop

♿ Facilities for visitors with disabilities

✋ Admission charges: Expensive (over $13), Moderate ($7–13), and Inexpensive (under $7)

⬌ Other nearby places of interest

❓ Other practical information

➤ Indicates the page where you will find a fuller description

ℹ Tourist information

ORGANIZATION

This guide is divided into six sections:
• Planning Ahead, Getting There
• Living San Francisco—San Francisco Now, San Francisco Then, Time to Shop, Out and About, Walks, San Francisco by Night
• San Francisco's Top 25 Sights
• San Francisco's Best—best of the rest
• Where to—detailed listings of restaurants, hotels, stores and nightlife
• Travel facts—packed with practical information

In addition, easy-to-read side panels provide fascinating extra facts and snippets, highlights of places to visit and invaluable practical advice.

The colors of the tabs on the page corners match the colors of the triangles aligned with the chapter names on the contents page opposite.

MAPS

The fold-out map in the wallet at the back of the book is a comprehensive street plan of San Francisco. The first (or only) map reference given for each attraction refers to this map. **The Top 25 locator maps** found on the inside front and back covers of the book itself are for quick reference. They show the Top 25 Sights, described on pages 26–50, which are clearly plotted by number (**1**–**25**, not page number) across the city. The second map reference given for the Top 25 Sights refers to this map.

Contents

Planning Ahead

WHEN TO GO

San Francisco's peak tourist months are July and August and hotels are busy. September and October are better times to visit, as the crowds have thinned and the weather is warm and sunny. Take a sweater and jacket for evening as fogs off the Pacific Ocean can chill the air.

TIME

San Francisco is on Pacific Standard Time, eight hours behind the UK and nine hours behind Western Europe.

AVERAGE DAILY MAXIMUM TEMPERATURES

JAN	FEB	MAR	APR	MAY	JUN	JUL	AUG	SEP	OCT	NOV	DEC
55°F	54°F	55°F	55°F	61°F	61°F	61°F	61°F	70°F	70°F	61°F	54°F
13°C	12°C	13°C	13°C	16°C	16°C	16°C	16°C	21°C	21°C	16°C	12°C

Spring (March to May) fogs usually only occur in the morning and have lifted by midday as the temperature rises.

Summer (June to August) weather is unpredictable. One day may be warm and sunny and the next a chilly fog appears in the morning and lingers through the evening.

Fall (September to November) sees the warmest and clearest days of the year.

Winter (December to February) rain can be heavy, especially in January. There are often torrential storms and it can rain for several days. Most rainfall occurs during winter.

6098635

WHAT'S ON

January/February *Chinese New Year*: Two weeks of Chinatown festivities; date depends on the lunar cycle.

March *St. Patrick's Day* (Mar 17): Irish and would-be-Irish dress in green for a parade on Market Street.

April *Cherry Blossom Festival*: Japantown celebrates Japanese art and culture.

May *Cinco de Mayo* (May 5): Mexican celebration centered in Mission District.

Bay to Breakers: Athletes and exhibitionists race from one side of the city to the other.

Carnaval: The Mission District fills with music, floats, costumes.

June *Gay Pride Freedom Day*: Huge march, usually starting or ending at Civic Center Plaza.

July *Independence Day* (Jul 4): Fireworks and a 50-cannon salute on the northern waterfront.

North Beach Festival: Music, food and sidewalk chalk art.

San Francisco Marathon: The country's third-largest marathon crosses Golden Gate Bridge.

September *San Francisco Blues Festival* (last weekend in Sep). An open-air celebration of blues.

October *Halloween Parade* (Oct 31): Outrageous costumes along Castro Street, plus an official celebration at Civic Center.

November *Day of the Dead* (Nov 2): Mexican tribute to the spirit world, with a parade through the Mission District.

Events Information
☎ 415/391–2000

4

SAN FRANCISCO ONLINE

At the heart of digital culture, San Francisco has excellent websites with regularly updated information on everything from the theater to local news, weather and gossip.

www.digitalcity.com/sanfrancisco/
www.sanfrancisco.citysearch.com

Professional reviews with local tips covering shops, restaurants, nightspots, museums, cinemas, theaters and more.

www.sfstation.com

Cutting-edge nightclubs, bars and stores.

www.theatrebayarea.org

Theater news and listings.

www.nps.gov

Factual information on the city's federally run parks, including Alcatraz.

www.gracecom.org

Details Grace Cathedral's history and provides a captivating virtual tour of the interior.

www.diggers.org

Tells the story of the proto-hippie Diggers, active in Haight-Ashbury in the mid-1960s and full of radical ideas even today.

www.sfgate.com

The *San Francisco Chronicle* website with dining, nightlife and events news.

www.sfbg.com/www.sfweekly.com

The influential websites of the free weekly papers, *San Francisco Bay Guardian* and *SF Weekly*.

www.sanfran.com

San Francisco magazine dispenses ideas for elegant shopping, dining and generally spending money around town.

www.511.org

Brings Bay Area travel, be it by car, bike, bus, train or plane, into a single site.

PRIME TRAVEL SITES

www.bart.gov/
www.sfmuni.com
Timetables, routes and fares.
www.flysfo.com/
www.flyoakland.com/www.sjc.org
Details travel to and from the airports.
www.ci.sf.ca.us
The city's administration provides more practical information.
www.fodors.com
A travel-planning site where you can research prices and weather, book tickets, cars and rooms and ask fellow travelers questions; links to other sites.

CYBERCAFÉS

Most hotels and many cafés and bars in San Francisco offer free or low-cost internet access. The following stand out in this fully wired city: **Galley Café** (✉ 1200 Mason Street ☎ 415/296–9932). Organic breads, gourmet coffee and free internet access. **Maggie Mud** (✉ 903 Cortland Avenue ☎ 415/641–5291). Free access is the excuse for sampling the 65 flavors of ice cream here. **Quetzal** (✉ 1234 Polk Street ☎ 415/673–4181). Organic coffees and a range of fruit smoothies.

Getting There

Visitors to San Francisco from outside the US must have a full passport and a return ticket. For countries participating in the Visa Waiver Program, a visa is not required, though you must fill out the green visa-waiver form issued on the plane. You are also required to fill out a customs form and an immigration form.

MONEY

The unit of currency is the dollar (=100 cents). Notes (bills) come in denominations of $1, $5, $10, $20, $50 and $100; coins are 25¢ (a quarter), 10¢ (a dime), 5¢ (a nickel) and 1¢ (a penny).

$5

$10

$50

$100

ARRIVING

There are direct flights to San Francisco from all over the world. The main airport is San Francisco International (SFO). Domestic airlines also serve Oakland Airport and San Jose International.

40 MILES (65KM)

Oakland Airport
17 miles (27km) to city center
Coach 1hr, $6–$12 one way ✈

SFO ✈
14 miles (23km) to city center
Coach 1hr, $14 one way
BART 30 mins, $4.95 one way

San Jose
45 miles (73km) to city center
Bus and train 80 mins, $5.25 one way ✈

FROM SFO

San Francisco International Airport (☎ 650/ 821–8211) is 14 miles (23km) south of the city. BART (☎ 415/989–2278) runs directly to the city from the airport, cost $4.95 and takes around 30 minutes. SFO Airporter coaches (☎ 650/ 246–8942) take visitors from the airport to the city every 20 minutes between 5am and 11pm, cost $14 one way, and take an hour to make the journey. Privately run mini buses such as SuperShuttle (☎ 650/558–8500) pick up from the traffic island outside and range from $13–$14 per person. A taxi into the city costs $35–$45.

FROM OAKLAND INTERNATONAL

Oakland (☎ 510/563–3300), which serves both domestic and international flights, is across the bay, 17 miles (27km) from the city. You travel into the city via I-880 and I-80; traffic on the Bay Bridge may make travel time longer. The Bay Transit Shuttle (☎ 510/714–4000) will get you to the city in about an hour, cost $6–$12 one way. Otherwise take the Air-Bart shuttle to the Coliseum/Oakland station, cost $2, and catch the next Bart to the city, cost around $3.

FROM SAN JOSE INTERNATIONAL

The city's third airport (☎ 408/277–4759), although about 45 miles (73km) south of downtown San Francisco, is well served by domestic carriers. Take the VTA Airport Flyer (route 10) to Santa Clara station and then CalTrain (☎ 800/660–4287) to the city, which takes about 80 minutes and costs $5.50.

ARRIVING BY BUS

Greyhound buses (☎ 0800/229–9424) into the city terminate at the Transbay Terminal, First and Mission streets.

ARRIVING BY TRAIN

Amtrak (☎ 800/872–7245) serves Emeryville west of the city, and provides free shuttle buses from there to San Francisco's Transbay Terminal.

GETTING AROUND

Much of San Francisco can be explored on foot but the city has an excellent system (➤ 91) of buses and cable cars, as well as the underground BART system, chiefly used for crossing the bay to Berkeley and Oakland. MUNI buses and metro trains (☎ 415/673–MUNI) serve the outer neighborhoods. Use taxis if you are in a rush, traveling late at night or want to pass quickly through edgy neighborhoods. Buses cover the entire city, operating 5am–1am; outside these hours Owl Service buses provide a reduced-frequency service on main routes. The flat fare is currently $1.25; to change buses on a single ride, ask the driver for a free transfer ticket. Exact change in coins is necessary and should be fed into the machine next to the driver when boarding.

Cable cars, more a tourist attraction than a practical means of getting around, operate on three routes between 6.30am and 12.30am: Powell–Mason and Powell–Hyde run between Market Street and Fisherman's Wharf, and California runs between Financial District and Nob Hill. Tickets cost $3 per ride and should be bought from the self-service machines at the end of each route, or from the conductor when you board.

HANDY HINT

A Muni Passport, which is valid on all MUNI buses, metro, trains and cable cars for one, three or seven days costs $9, $15 or $20 respectively. Muni Passports can be bought at the Visitor Information Center (➤ 90).

VISITORS WITH DISABILITIES

Aside from its steep hills, San Francisco is generally a good city for visitors using a wheelchair, with ramped public buildings and accessible buses, BART stations and taxis. Some hotels have roll-in showers, and some have Braille signage. For details, see *Access San Francisco*, a free annually updated booklet published by Access Northern California (www.accessnca.com), available from the Convention & Visitors Bureau. Also contact the Mayor's Office on Disability ✉ 401 Van Ness Avenue, Room 300, San Francisco, CA 94102 ☎ 415/554–6789; www. ci.sf.ca.us/sfmod

Living
San Francisco

San Francisco Now

Above: *Victorian houses on Russian Hill*
Right: *Evening ice skating, the Embarcadero*
Top far right: *Chinese New Year celebrations*
Far right: *San Francisco Museum of Modern Art*

Since the Gold Rush transformed San Francisco almost overnight from a hamlet into a city in the 1850s, it has been different from other cities. The anything-goes atmosphere of the early days forged a lasting and pervasive atmosphere of tolerance and a welcoming attitude toward change. Home to a multitude of races, religions and cultures with a long history of immigration, San Francisco is intensely cosmopolitan. As such, the city also gives a look into the multicultural future of California, the first state in the country without an ethnic majority.

San Francisco has frequently set the nation's cultural and social pace. It witnessed the birth of the 1950s' Beat generation, of the hippie era in the 1960s, of the

HAIGHT-ASHBURY AND THE 1960s

• Haight-Ashbury (► 52) already held a remarkable collection of alternative lifestyles in the mid-1960s, when local use of a then legal hallucinogenic drug, LSD, encouraged the idea of a psychedelic revolution. By 1967, sensationalist publicity had encouraged thousands of what became termed "hippies" to colonize the area's spacious but rundown Victorian homes. Local bands such as the Grateful Dead and Jefferson Airplane achieved global recognition but soon left the neighborhood, which declined sharply until re-inventing itself as an offbeat shopping district during the 1990s.

UPBEAT MOOD

• Despite economic gloom, major building projects, among them Yerba Buena Gardens, which has drawn together museums and cultural centers, and Pacific Bay Park, a home for baseball's San Francisco Giants, have bought a sense of optimism to the city.

Above: *San Francisco gay parade*
Top right: *Sunset over the rugged coastline outside the city*

JOHN McLAREN

• Born in Scotland in 1846, John McLaren moved to California in the 1870s and became supervisor of Golden Gate Park in 1887. So well known did the "tyrannical and capricious" Scot become that his birthday was celebrated as a civic event and a special law was passed in 1917 enabling him to work beyond retirement age. He died in 1943.

gay and lesbian liberation movement in the 1970s. Through the 1990s, its multimedia and internet companies set the pace for the global information revolution along with those of Silicon Valley, an hour's drive away.

Ironically, the dot-com explosion that energized the city and transformed its economy also looked set to destroy its tradition of offering affordable housing to all income groups. Homes were converted to high-rent loft-style apartments for newly wealthy internet entrepreneurs forced many on lower and middle incomes out of town.

With the city's increasing dependance on dot-com finance, the downturn in the e-economy in 2000 had a major impact and many in the industry had to reassess their priorities, which created a surge of unemployed dot-commers. During 2001, more people left the Bay area than settled in, bringing a falling population for the first time since the 1970s. During 2003, even the Golden Gate Bridge was asking for donations toward its upkeep in boxes placed along its span.

Left: *Golden Gate bridge is often shrouded in fog*
Above: *Transamerica Pyramid, the tallest building in San Francisco*

San Franciscans can take heart from living in a city that retains such distinctive traditional features as cable cars, steep streets, morning fogs and intricate Victorian architecture, and a proliferation of informal cafés where smoking may be banned but coffee in many exotic forms is served to discerning drinkers. And they can also celebrate continuing to be different from the rest of the US, not least when mayor Gavin Newsome gave City Hall the green light during 2004 to perform gay marriage ceremonies, polarizing opinion across the nation.

THE "F" WORD

● The worst mistake a newcomer to San Francisco is likely to make is calling the city "Frisco," a term known locally as the "F" word. You can earn considerable respect by using insider lingo—simply call San Francisco "the city."

THE EARTHQUAKE AND FIRE OF 1906

● Striking at 5.12am on April 18, 1906, what became the great San Francisco earthquake measured 7.9 on the modern Richter scale but caused relatively minor damage. By rupturing gas and water mains however, it caused fires to break out and burn uncontrolled for three days. Only a change in wind direction halted the blaze, by which time 3,000 acres (1,215ha) of San Francisco had been devastated, 250,000 of the city's 400,000 inhabitants had been rendered homeless and 300 were dead (although more recent reports suggest as many as 3,000 had perished). The quake, along the San Andreas Fault, was a forceful reminder of the area's geological instability; the recovery highlighted the city's regenerative powers, which are symbolized by the city's official emblem, the phoenix.

13

Top: *A crab vendor, Fisherman's Wharf*
Top right: *wildly colorful Haight Street*
Above: *The "Painted Ladies," Steiner Street*
Above right: *Dragon dancers, Chinese New Year parade*

With 16 million annual arrivals, San Francisco is the most visited city in the US, and tourism has been a major source of income since the 1970s. As a result, the city is visitor-friendly, and opportunities to explore beneath the surface are plentiful. Boat trips, bus tours and guided walks let you learn about San Francisco's communities, neighborhoods, history, architecture and enjoy its stupendous natural setting with ease.

Small by world standards, San Francisco houses around 790,000 people and occupies a compact peninsula that is not only scenically spectacular but also prevents sprawl. The area divides into several neighborhoods all linked by

ALICE WATERS

• Berkeley's doyenne of food, Alice Waters, celebrated her restaurant's (Chez Panisse) 30th birthday in 2001, but her famously simple fare isn't showing signs of age. Pioneering the concept of using seasonal, organic ingredients, Alice has influenced chefs domestically and abroad with her unpretentious menus that allow the fresh, local ingredients to assume the starring role. Rumblings of retirement have been heard across the Bay so don't wait another three decades to make your reservations.

public transportation and many, including perennially visitor-pleasing Chinatown and North Beach, are easy to walk between and through, and well within reach of downtown, the business hub and Fisherman's Wharf, the only area dominated by tourists.

Despite its international renown, San Francisco has rarely wielded major economic or political power. However, it does seem to relish people power—its citizens, who shun cars and depend on the public transit system, are known to march on City Hall to protest a fare rise of just a few cents—and strives to improve what is regarded as an above average quality of life.

The rise and rise of Yerba Buena Gardens, the re-development of Union Street and the on-going improvement of the Embarcadero, promise to create a city center that goes some way to matching San Francisco's natural setting. Meanwhile, it is hoped that the linking of a new-look San Francisco airport to the BART transit system will create an encouraging first impression for new arrivals.

VITAL STATISTICS

• San Francisco is 2,930 miles (4,726km) from New York, 397 miles (640km) from Los Angeles, 6,010 miles (9,694km) from London and 6,094 miles (9,829km) from Berlin.

• San Francisco's area of 46.38sq miles (119sq km) is occupied by a population of 790,000.

• San Francisco's steepest streets are Filbert between Leavenworth and Hyde and 22nd Street between Church and Vicksburg, each with a 31.5 percent gradient.

15

San Francisco Then

Above: *prospecting for gold*

EMPEROR NORTON

Wearing epaulettes and a cockaded hat, Joshua Norton proclaimed himself "Emperor of the United States and Protector of Mexico" in 1856 and was effectively accepted as such throughout San Francisco. On his death in 1880, flags flew at half mast and his funeral was attended by the mayor.

"BEATNIKS"

The 1957 publication of Allen Ginsberg's poem *Howl* by North Beach bookstore-publisher City Lights made the area a prime destination for what longtime San Francisco Chronicle columnist Herb Caen labeled "beatniks."

1769 The Spanish discover San Francisco Bay.

1821 Mexico takes California from Spain.

1846 The United States takes control of California by force from Mexico.

1849 California Gold Rush begins. San Francisco's population soars from 812 to 20,000 as the city becomes the commercial center for miners.

1873 First cable car runs along Clay Street.

1906 The city is ruined by earthquake and fire.

1915 The Panama Pacific Exposition symbolizes the city's recovery from the earthquake.

1937 Golden Gate Bridge is completed.

1941 US entry into World War II stimulates war industries and brings an influx of military and civilian personnel to the city. Employment in the ship-yards grows from 4,000 to 260,000.

1945 50 countries sign the United Nations charter in the SF Opera House.

1964 Students at Berkeley form the non-violent Free Speech Movement and

instigate the first of many campus revolts in the US.

1966 The militant African-American group, the Black Panthers, form in Oakland.

1967 The "Summer Of Love": Young people arrive from across the country and Haight-Ashbury's hippie population grows from 7,000 to 75,000.

1989 The Loma Prieta earthquake (7.1 on the Richter scale) kills 67 people and closes the Bay Bridge for a month.

1995 Willine Brown becomes the city's first black mayor.

1996 San Francisco becomes the first local government to sue the tobacco industry.

1998 It becomes illegal to smoke in public indoor spaces.

1999 The $3.3 billion injected into San Francisco-based dotcom companies re-shapes city's economic base.

2002 Continuing decline of the e-economy brings financial uncertainty.

2004 Much publicized same-sex weddings take place at City Hall as 1,600 gay couples apply for licences.

Above left to right:
Devastation after the
1906 earthquake;
Golden Gate Bridge under
construction;
rock concert poster from
the sixties

GAY PROTEST

In 1977 Harvey Milk became the nation's first openly gay male to be elected to public office. The following year, Milk and Mayor George Moscone were assassinated at City Hall by a former city politician, Dan White. The lightweight five-year prison sentence bestowed on White prompted the White Night Riots; predominantly gay demonstrators marched on City Hall, causing $1 million dollars worth of damage.

17

Time to Shop

Below: *A psychedelic shop front*
Below right: *Anchorage Shopping Center*

While San Francisco may not be in the same shopping league as London, Paris or New York, many prefer its slower pace and are surprised by the array of paraphernalia to be found. Each neighborhood reflects its style in the clothes, furnishings, antiques, books, food

STYLE OVER SUBSTANCE

"Design matters" proclaimed the San Francisco magazine *One*. The publication lasted less than a year, but the slogan is still relevant. Design has always played an important role in San Francisco. Designer Paul Frank puts his ubiquitous monkey on just about everything, from T-shirts to bar stools at the Paul Frank Store (✉ 262 Sutter Street ☎ 415/374–2758). Furniture is also an art form in some San Francisco stores. At Limn (✉ 290 Townsend Street ☎ 415/543–5466) check out the work of graphic designer Fabien Baron, who created the furniture line for Capellini. New Deal (✉ 1632B Market Street ☎ 415/552– 6208) has furniture, lighting and artworks to enhance any design-conscious pad.

and souvenirs on offer, making shopping an enjoyable accompanient to exploring these different areas.

Various knick-knacks decorated with the Golden Gate Bridge, Alcatraz or the words "I Left My Heart in San Francisco" predominate among the souvenirs widely found in Fisherman's Wharf and the smaller sprinkling of trinket outlets in Chinatown and Downtown. Those of a nervous disposition might choose to avoid the many jokey earthquake-related items, while Ghirardelli chocolate makes a good gift for anyone with a sweet tooth.

The produce of California's numerous wineries is stocked throughout the city. Many neighborhood outlets carry local labels such as Dry Creek, Geyser Peak or Lambert Bridge and have weekly drop-in wine tastings. Having chosen your wine head to the local bakery for a loaf of Boudin's sourdough bread (► 67). The Boudin tradition continues with the same distinctive sourdough that arrived in San Francisco during the Gold Rush. A local specialty is fresh clam chowder served in a sourbread bowl.

In Chinatown and the less-tourist-visited Asian shops on Clement Street in the Richmond

Below left: *Borders book and music store*
Below: *Union Square shopping complex*

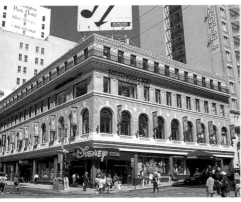

District are rich pickings for amateur cooks looking to extend their stocks of utensils or to select from an array of otherwise hard-to-find spices and herbs.

Rich with new and secondhand bookstores, San Francisco was a fulcrum of the 1950s Beat explosion and is the best place to find the definitive stock of Beat and Beat-related literature and criticism. Haight-Ashbury's original hippies may have moved on but the tie-dyed T-shirts and other totems of flower power are still available along Haight Street, which is also the best stop in the city for wacky, vintage clothing and obscure CDs and vinyl.

Other noted neighborhood shopping streets include Chestnut Street in the Marina District and Union and Fillmore streets in Pacific Heights, all proffering generally smart clothing, antiques and household items. In North Beach, Grant Avenue has outlets for bric-a-brac and unusual crafts as well as silks and pearls.

MUSEUM STORES

Alongside posters and art books, the San Francisco Museum of Modern Art offers jewelry, lamps and inventive toys such as an architect-designed update of the dollhouse. The Exploratorium has nature and science books and quirky science-related items including the lightening machine, powered by household static electricity.

Out and About

Above left to right:
*Café in North Beach,
where many Italians
have settled; the
Japanese Tea Gardens,
Golden Gate Park;
Oakland Museum*

WALKING TOURS

City Guides (☎ 415/557–4266) has free daily tours to City Hall, Haight-Ashbury, Nob Hill, Sutro Heights Park, the mansions of Pacific Heights, and the murals of the Mission District. The Wok Wiz (☎ 650/355–9657) offers Chinatown three-hour tours that take in herb shops, artists and historic sites with an optional lunch that unravels the mysteries of *dim sum*.

ORGANIZED SIGHTSEEING

If your time is limited, opt for a guided bus tour. Tower Tours (☎ 888/657–4520) has a half-day tour of the city that can be combined with a cruise in the bay. Gray Line Tours (☎ 888/428–6937) has both a half-day tour and an evening tour that includes a walk around Chinatown and an optional dinner.

ITINERARIES
ALCATRAZ TO TELEGRAPH HILL

To avoid the crowds take the first ferry from Fisherman's Wharf to the former island prison of Alcatraz (➤ 38). Return from Alcatraz, then walk or take public transportation from Fisherman's Wharf to North Beach (➤ 53), where you can explore the cafés and bookstores, the North Beach Museum (➤ 55), Washington Square (➤ 58) and the Church of Sts. Peter and Paul (➤ 54). Continue to Telegraph Hill's Coit Tower (➤ 59) and the flower-edged Filbert Steps (➤ 62).

HAIGHT–ASHBURY TO GOLDEN GATE PARK

Start the day in Haight-Ashbury (➤ 52), where you can tour some of the streets and browse Haight Street's unusual stores. Take lunch in a local café (➤ 64–65).
Walk from Haight-Ashbury into Golden Gate Park (➤ 27). The Conservatory of Flowers, the Japanese Tea Garden, the Aids Memorial Grove and the California Academy of Sciences (➤ 30) are all within strolling distance. To see more of

the park, rent a bicycle from one of the outlets on Stanyan Street.

EXCURSIONS
BERKLEY & OAKLAND
Take BART to Berkeley then walk to the University of California campus (► 50) and explore its museums and public buildings. From the campus, cross onto Telegraph Avenue, lined with lively restaurants and bookstores. Continue by BART to Oakland. Visit the Oakland Museum (► 49), then walk north to take in the view across Lake Merritt. After touring the 19th-century Camron-Stanford House beside the lake, take BART or a bus to Oakland's Chinatown and the stores and attractions of Jack London Square. Return to San Francisco by ferry for a dramatic view of the city skyline.

SONOMA VALLEY
Drive across the Golden Gate Bridge and continue north on US 101 through San Rafael to Sonoma. While in the town explore the Sonoma Mission and the other restored historic buildings and stores around Sonoma Plaza.
Continue to the Buena Vista Winery, then head north to the hamlet of Glen Ellen and tour Jack London State Historic Park, former home of the writer whose name it bears. Continue north to Kenwood, where there are more wineries, including Château St. Jean. Return to Sonoma and turn west along Highway 116 to Petaluma Adobe State Historic Park.

Above: *A church in the Sonoma Valley used for a scene in Alfred Hitchcock's 1963 movie* The Birds

INFORMATION

BERKELEY & OAKLAND
☎ BART information 510/465–2278; Berkeley Campus information 510/642–5215; Oakland Convention & Visitors Bureau 510/839–9000; Oakland–San Francisco ferry Blue & Gold Fleet 415/705–5555
🚇 Berkeley: Berkeley; Oakland: Lake Merritt for the museum and 12th Street for Chinatown

SONOMA VALLEY
☎ Buena Vista Winery 800/265–1472; Jack London State Historic Park 707/938–5216; Château St. Jean 707/833–4134; Petaluma State Historic Park 707/762–4871

Walks

INFORMATION

Distance Approx 1.5 miles (2.5km)
Time 2 hours
Start point ★ Westin Street, Francis Hotel, Union Square
🚇 K5
🚌 2, 3, 4, 6, 38, 71; Powell–Hyde and Powell–Mason cable cars
End point North Beach
🚇 K3/4

```
0                    600 m
0                    600 yards
```

UNION SQUARE TO NORTH BEACH

Begin in Union Square in the lobby of the Westin St. Francis Hotel (► 86), where the grandfather clock has long been a renowned San Franciscan meeting place.

Leave the hotel and cross Union Square. Note the square's Dewey Monument, with its bronze figure of Victory reputedly modeled on Alma Spreckels (► 28). Leave the square, crossing Stockton Street for Maiden Lane (► 62). In Maiden Lane, note the Circle Gallery. From Maiden Lane, walk north along Kearny Street past the Bank of America Center, and turn left onto California Street, walking uphill and crossing the street for Old St. Mary's Church.

Stroll along Grant Avenue into the heart of Chinatown. Turn onto Clay Street and visit the Chinese Historical Society of America. Afterward return along Clay Street to Waverly Place (► 62) and the Tien Hou Temple. Turn right along Washington Street to Portsmouth Square, noting the memorial to Robert Louis Stevenson on the north side, and go straight on for a visit to the Transamerica Pyramid (► 47). Walk, or take a bus, along Columbus Avenue for North Beach and lunch.

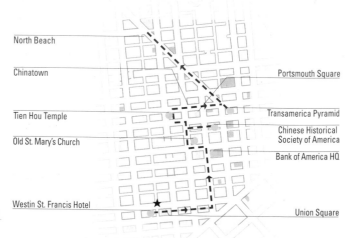

North Beach

Chinatown

Portsmouth Square

Tien Hou Temple

Transamerica Pyramid

Chinese Historical Society of America

Old St. Mary's Church

Bank of America HQ

Westin St. Francis Hotel

Union Square

NORTH BEACH TO THE TRANSAMERICA PYRAMID

After lunch, browse around City Lights, a bookstore pivotal to the 1950s Beat Generation. Alongside, Jack Kerouac Street was named for one of the movement's leading figures, and the adjacent Vesuvio (► 84) was a popular hangout. Across Columbus Avenue, note the Condor Bistro, formerly the Condor Club and, in 1964, scene of the first topless act in the United States (commemorated by a plaque).

Cross to Stockton Street for the North Beach Museum. Return along Vallejo Street to Columbus Avenue, crossing the latter for the Church of St. Francis of Assisi, founded in 1849 and the first Catholic church in California since the Spanish missions. Continue north, browsing around Grant Avenue's unusual stores. Turn onto Union Street for Washington Square and the Church of Sts. Peter and Paul. Climb Filbert Street (or use bus 39) to reach Coit Tower, then descend the Filbert Steps. In Montgomery Street, note the art-deco apartment building at number 1360, which was featured, with Humphrey Bogart and Lauren Bacall, in the 1947 film *Dark Passage*. Then follow Montgomery Street south to return to North Beach.

INFORMATION

Distance 1.25 miles (2km)
Time 1½–2 hours
Start point ★ City Lights bookstore
🚻 K4
🚌 15, 41, 83
End point Montgomery Street
🚻 L4

BEAT LANDMARKS

Devotees of the 1950s Beat Generation might like to extend their walk to 1010 Montgomery Street, Allen Ginsberg's home where he completed *Howl*. Ginsberg read the poem in public for the first time at 3119 Fillmore Street, Pacific Heights. Jack Kerouac, meanwhile, wrote parts of *On The Road* in the loft of 29 Russell Street, Russian Hill.

0 ———— 600 m
0 ———— 600 yards

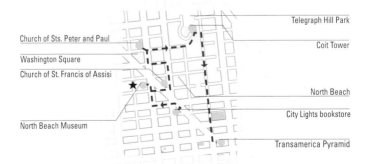

Church of Sts. Peter and Paul
Washington Square
Church of St. Francis of Assisi
North Beach Museum

Telegraph Hill Park
Coit Tower
North Beach
City Lights bookstore
Transamerica Pyramid

23

San Francisco by Night

Above: *Broadway offers a mix of cafés and adult entertainment*
Above right: *The illuminated downtown skyline*

OPENING TIMES

Most discos, clubs and bars (➤ 82–83) open nightly, from around 9pm, but are busiest around midnight, closing at 2am on week nights (later on weekends).

UP, UP, AND AWAY

For a truly spectacular night, take an evening helicopter flight. San Francisco Helicopter Tours (☎ 800/400–2404) offer a package that includes a flight, followed by dinner and dancing aboard the Hornblower yacht as it sails around the bay.

Late-opening stores, restaurants, bars and spectacular views all enliven San Francisco after dark. Prime evening areas include North Beach, Chinatown and the Union Square area. SoMa has the latest nightclubs and on Fisherman's Wharf nightlife is designed for tourists. San Francisco offers a number of alluring possibilities for a pre-dinner experience in interesting surroundings before taking a short appetite-sharpening stroll to a restaurant.

TAKE IN THE LIGHTS

Take the bus or climb the hill leading to Coit Tower (➤ 59; open until 6.30pm only in summer), for a view across the Bay area. Even when the tower is closed, views from the adjoining park are worth the effort. Walk down the hill for dinner in North Beach or Chinatown.

DRINK WITH A VIEW

Relax with a cocktail as you take in the view from the 21st-floor Starlight Room of the Sir Francis Drake Hotel (➤ 83) and glide across the floor to the silky sounds of the Starlight Orchestra. Alternatively have a pre-dinner tipple at the Carnelian Room (➤ 83) on the 52nd floor of the Bank of America Center (➤ 56), then walk north into Chinatown or North Beach for dinner. Or try the Marriott Hotel's (➤ 56) 39th-floor View Lounge from which it's an easy walk to SoMa or Union Square for dinner.

SAN FRANCISCO's
top 25 sights

The sights are shown on the maps on the inside front cover and inside back cover, numbered **1**–**25** across the city

Golden Gate NRA

INFORMATION

- A–J 1–10 and off map; Locator map B1
- GGNRA Headquarters: Building 201, Fort Mason Center
- Cissy Field Center 415/561–4700
- Daylight hours only recommended. Cissy Field Center Wed–Sun 9–5
- 5, 18, 19, 28, 29, 30, 31, 32, 38, 42, 48, 76
- Range from none to excellent according to location; for details ☎ 415/441–5706
- Free
- Golden Gate Bridge (➤ 29), Fort Mason Center (➤ 35), National Maritime Museum (➤ 55), Marina Green (➤ 58), Sutro Heights Park (➤ 59), San Francisco Zoo (➤ 60)
- Ranger-led tours

An enormous swath of mostly undeveloped land lying within the city and extending northward across the Golden Gate Bridge, the Golden Gate National Recreation Area is a wonderful reminder of how open and wild most of California is.

Creation From the cliffs of Fort Funston in the south to the hills of Marin County in the north, the Golden Gate National Recreation Area (GGNRA) bestows federal protection on a long, slender chunk of San Francisco's coastline. The area's 75,000 acres (30,364ha), which lie in separate pockets and often lack clearly marked boundaries, were created in 1972 by the amalgamation of city parks, private land and former military-owned areas. Abandoned fortifications include a Civil War fort (Fort Point, which is located beneath the Golden Gate Bridge) and a massive World War II cannon at Baker Beach.

Exploration Much of Golden Gate NRA is best explored on foot. Start at the Cliff House, close to the sea lion-frequented Seal Rocks. Walk the blustery coastal trail that weaves through the coarsely vegetated hillsides, which rise steeply above the tiny beach of Lands End and the forbidding waters of the Golden Gate. All vestiges of the city are entirely hidden until the appearance of the Golden Gate Bridge. This route also brings views of the isolated China Beach, named for the Chinese fishermen of the Gold Rush era who lived in shacks beside it. China Beach is one of the few San Francisco beaches that is safe for swimming, while the more accessible Baker Beach, where swimming is not permitted, is the perfect spot for a rest.

Golden Gate Park

Once a desolate stretch of sand dunes, Golden Gate Park is now a massive slab of greenery holding several museums. It's also a stage from which San Francisco, and its jogging, kite-flying, roller-skating population, presents its playful side to the world.

Acres of fun Some 3 miles (5km) long and half a mile (1km) wide, Golden Gate Park is one of the world's largest urban parks. Secreted within its 1,000 acres (405ha) are the De Young Museum (▶ 30), the Conservatory of Flowers, a polo field, golf course, archery range, botanical garden, lakes, waterfalls, two windmills and bison paddock. Yet there is still sufficient space to become hopelessly lost amid tree-shrouded lanes and footpaths.

On foot The park is too large to cover entirely on foot but the eastern half is fine for strolling. Here you will find the redstone McLaren Lodge, former office of the park's creator and now an information center (maps are essential), and the AIDS Memorial Grove, a 15-acre (6-ha) wooded grove and scene of private services following the loss of a loved one to AIDS. Nearby is the Conservatory of Flowers with its tropical vegetation, the Japanese Tea Garden, with azaleas, cherry trees and a carp-filled pond linked by pathways. West of the Tea Garden a road encircles Stow Lake, at the center of which Strawberry Hill rises to a 400-ft (122-m) summit.

HIGHLIGHTS

- Conservatory of Flowers
- Japanese Tea Garden
- Stow Lake

INFORMATION

- ✚ A–F 7–8; Locator map B2
- ✉ Bordered by Great Highway, Lincoln Way, Fulton Street and Stanyan Street
- ☎ 415/831–2700
- 🕐 Daylight hours only recommended
- 🍴 Tea at Japanese Tea Garden
- 🚌 5, 7, 18, 21, 28, 29, 44, 71
- ♿ Good
- 🎟 Free
- 🔗 De Young Museum (▶ 30)
- ℹ Park Visitor Center
  ✉ Beach Chalet, between Fulton Street and Lincoln Avenue
  ☎ 415/751–2766
  🕐 Daily 9–6

Golden Gate Park: Old North Windmill and the Queen Wilhelmina Tulip Garden

Palace of the Legion of Honor

HIGHLIGHTS

- *Eiffel Tower*, Seurat
- *Water Lilies*, Monet
- *The Tribute Money*, Rubens
- *St. John the Baptist*, El Greco
- *Thinker*, Rodin
- *The Shades*, Rodin
- *Holocaust* sculpture, Segal
- *Old Man* and *Old Woman*, De la Tour
- *Man With a Broken Nose*, Rodin
- View of Golden Gate

INFORMATION

- B5; Locator map A2
- Lincoln Park
- 415/750–3600; recorded information 415/863–3330
- Tue–Sun 9.30–5
- Simple café
- 18
- Good
- Moderate; free every Tue
- Golden Gate National Recreation Area (➤ 26)
- Free tours daily

Rodin and San Francisco may seem an unlikely combination, but fans of the sculptor enjoy a visit to this hill-top building that has many of his works amid a fine collection of European art.

Sugar money The collection in the California Palace of the Legion of Honor (modeled on the Légion d'Honneur Museum in Paris) was started in the 1910s by Alma Spreckels, wife of millionaire San Franciscan sugar magnate, Adolph. Already passionate about European art, Alma met Rodin in Paris and began a lasting interest in his work. Her husband, meanwhile, was motivated to open an art museum through his bitter rivalry with another prominent San Franciscan family, the De Youngs, who had founded the M. H. De Young Memorial Museum (➤ 30).

The collections *The Shades* and *Thinker* stand in the grounds, and some 70 other Rodin works are inside the museum. The general galleries, meanwhile, are arranged in a chronological sequence from the medieval period to the early 20th century, with the highlights mostly from the 18th and 19th centuries. Downstairs, the Achenbach Foundation for Graphic Arts holds over 100,000 prints and some 3,000 drawings from artists as diverse as Albrecht Dürer and Georgia O'Keeffe, and selections are shown in short-term exhibitions (otherwise by appointment). Outside, beside the parking lot, be sure to see George Segal's *Holocaust* sculpture.

Golden Gate Bridge

Named for the entrance to San Francisco Bay rather than its color, Golden Gate Bridge must be the most recognizable, and the most beautiful, of all the bridges in the United States.

Artful engineering The bridge is a remarkable feat of artistry as well as engineering. The construction overcame the exceptional depth and strong currents of the Golden Gate, while the simple but inspired design allows it to sit with panache between the city and the wild hillsides of Marin County, its upper portions often evocatively shrouded in fog.

Loathed then loved A bond issue of $35 million was authorized in 1930 to finance the bridge's construction amid great antipathy from San Franciscans, many of whom feared that it would result in a loss of the natural beauty of the Golden Gate. An early design by the project's chief engineer, Joseph B. Strauss, was likened to "two grotesque steel beetles emerging from either bank." The design eventually adopted is thought to have been the work of one or more of Strauss's assistants. The affection that the bridge now enjoys among city dwellers was confirmed in 1987 when 200,000 people filed onto it to mark the 50th anniversary of its opening; their gathering caused the central span to drop by 10ft (3.5m).

Fatal attraction On a more downbeat note, the Golden Gate Bridge has become a noted spot for suicides. The first occurred three months after the bridge's opening and since then 1,000 people have ended their lives by jumping the 220ft (67m) from the central span to the raging waters beneath, their bodies usually carried out to the Pacific by the swift currents.

DID YOU KNOW

- Weight of steel in construction: 100,000 tons
- Length including approaches: 7 miles (11km)
- Actual bridge length: 6,450ft (1,966m)
- Length of central span: 4,200ft (1,280m)
- Height above water: 220ft (67m) at low tide
- Height of towers: 46ft (14m)
- Length of cables: 80,000 miles (129,032km)
- Color: International Orange, the color most easily distinguishable in fog
- Gallons of paint used annually: 5,000 (22,727L)
- Annual vehicle crossings: 42 million

INFORMATION

- D1–D3; Locator map B1
- Open to pedestrians daily 5am–9pm (6am–6pm in winter)
- 28, 29, 76
- Good at observation platform
- Free for pedestrians and cyclists. Moderate toll for city-bound drivers
- Golden Gate National Recreation Area (➤ 26)

29

de Young Museum

HIGHLIGHTS

- Diebenkorn's *Ocean Park #116*
- Bierstadt's *Storm in the Rocky Mountains*
- Bierstadt's *A View of Donner Lake, California*
- Anshutz's *The Ironworker's Noontime*
- Copley's *1763 Mrs. Daniel Sargent*
- Vanderlyn's *Marius Amidst the ruins of Carthage*
- Singer Sargent's *A Dinner Table at Night*
- Philadelphia High Chest of Drawers
- Shaker crafts

INFORMATION

- E7; Locator map C2
- Golden Gate Park
- 415/750–3600; recorded information 415/863–3330
- Wed–Sun 10–5; 10–8.45 first Wed of month
- Excellent café
- 44
- Excellent
- Moderate; includes California Palace of the Legion of Honor if visited on same day. Free first Wed and Sat am of month
- Golden Gate Park (➤ 27)
- Free tours daily. Lectures, films

From Anatolian prayer rugs to the dresses of Yves Saint-Laurent, this museum stocks diverse exhibits from around the world but the exemplary collections of American painting and decorative art are the main draw.

Paintings After several years of waiting in great anticipation, the de Young Museum returned home to Golden Gate Park in October 2005, re-opening in an architecturally stunning new buidling. After society portraits by John Singleton Copley and his 18th-century contemporaries, the paintings reveal the growing self-confidence of American artists and the lessening importance of European trends. By the mid-1800s, many American artists were taking inspiration from the newly-settled West: The landscapes of Albert Bierstadt and the sculpture of Frederick Remington evoke the period's celebratory mood of expansion. By contrast, Richard Diebenkorn's work is a strikingly Californian contribution to 1960s and 1970s contemporary art.

Furnishings The furniture, too, reflects the US's historic shift from colony to nation as it moves from English and Dutch armchairs used in New England settlements of 1670 to an elegant Federal-period parlor from 1805 Massachusetts. The flowing curves of the Queen Anne style were popular during the colonial period but by the time of the revolution, American craftsmen had acquired the skills and creativity to evolve a new and distinctive look, adding unique rococo touches. Philadelphia emerged above Boston and New York as the center of the craft, and a grand 1780 Philadelphia High Chest provides an excellent example of the period.

San Francisco Columbarium

One way to convince San Franciscans you know more about their city than they do is to tell them about the Columbarium, one of the city's most architecturally noteworthy buildings, but one most locals are unaware of.

The moving dead An elegant, three-story Victorian rotunda decorated with stained glass, the Columbarium (a final resting place for urns holding the ashes of the deceased) was designed by British architect Bernard Cahill and opened in 1898. By 1937, it stood in the heart of a 3-acre (1.5ha) cemetery in which an estimated 10,000 people were buried. That year, however, concerns for public health resulted in cemeteries being declared illegal in San Francisco; the graves (except for those at Mission Dolores and the Presidio) were exhumed and their contents moved out of the city.

The interior of the Columbarium

Notable niches Declared a memorial, the Columbarium itself was spared demolition but, with cremations being outlawed, it was left to decay. Restoration of the handsome structure began in 1980, and its empty niches were once again put on sale. Guided tours focus on the architecture, but even a swift glance at the niches reveals Eddys, Turks and other once-illustrious families who gave their names to city streets.

DID YOU KNOW?

- Architect: Bernard Cahill
- Year completed: 1898
- Original owners: Oddfellows Cemetery
- Subsequent owners: Bay City Cemeteries Association (1930), Cypress Abbey (1935), Neptune Society (1980)
- Number of niches: 30,000
- Number of unoccupied niches: 10,000
- Most expensive currently available niche: $56,000
- Least expensive currently available niche: $700
- Most unusual niche adornment: a set of miniature golf clubs

INFORMATION

- F6; Locator map C2
- 1 Loraine Court
- 415/771–0717
- Daily 10–1
- 33, 38, 50
- None
- Free
- Temple Emanu-El (➤ 54)
- Tours run periodically

Exploratorium

HIGHLIGHTS

- Tactile Dome
- Wave Organ
- *Alien Voices*
- Sound and Hearing
- *Tornado*
- Triple Eye Lightstick
- Distorted Room
- Shadow Box
- Vision, Color and Light
- Golden Gate Videodisc

INFORMATION

www.exploratorium.edu

⊞ G3; Locator map C1

✉ 3601 Lyon Street

☎ 415/563–7337;
recorded information
415/ex-plore;
Tactile Dome reservations
415/561–0362

◉ Daily 10–5

🍴 Reasonable cafeteria

🚌 28, 30

♿ Excellent

▣ Moderate; free 1st Wed
of month. Tactile Dome
moderate separate fee

↔ Palace of Fine Arts
(► 33), Marina Green
(► 58)

Undoubtedly the best place in San Francisco to amuse young minds with low boredom thresholds, the Exploratorium set the pace for hands-on museums across the US and also contains much to stimulate adults.

Questions and answers Founded by Frank Oppenheimer, who worked alongside his more famous brother, Robert, on the development of the atomic bomb in the 1940s, the Exploratorium occupies a single vast hall and has 650 hands-on, interactive exhibits designed to illustrate and explain the fundamentals of natural science and human perception in a user-friendly environment. Helpful red-jacketed "explainers" stroll around answering questions, and new exhibits are developed in a workshop open to public view. The odd bits of statuary you might spot gathering dust in the corners are remnants of the building's original role as part of the Palace of Fine Arts (► 33).

Innovative art and science Be they crackling tesla coils or coupled resonant pendulums, the permanent exhibits stand alongside a series of temporary (though usually long-term) installations. These have included Seeing, a multifaceted gathering exploring how humans interpret visual information and Traits of Life, an interactive presentation on the essentials of biology. An innovative artist-in-residence program has resulted in many imaginative artworks based on scientific themes. The Exploratorium's most popular item (and one that requires advance reservations) is the Tactile Dome, a dark "tunnel" from which participants can leave only by feeling their way out on their hands and knees.

Palace of Fine Arts

Together with the Golden Gate Bridge and City Hall, the Palace of Fine Arts is one of the most beautiful structures in San Francisco. Remarkably, it was intentionally built as a ruin and serves no practical purpose whatsoever.

Architects' playtime In 1915, ostensibly to mark the opening of the Panama Canal, San Francisco announced its recovery from the devastation of the 1906 earthquake and fire by staging the Panama Pacific International Exposition. A group of noted architects was commissioned to erect temporary structures to house the Expo on land reclaimed from the bay. One of the architects was Bernard Maybeck, and it was his Palace of Fine Arts more than any other building that captured the imagination of the Expo's 20 million visitors. Although it was intended as a temporary structure and was built mostly of plaster and chicken wire, the Palace of Fine Arts aroused such public affection that it was preserved and then, in the 1960s, replicated in concrete at a cost of $7.5 million.

Art in ruins Maybeck designed a Roman ruin, using a classical domed rotunda as the structure's centerpiece and flanking this with a fragmented colonnade. Each group of columns was topped by weeping maidens and decorated by aimless stairways and huge urns. The intention was to instill a sense of "moderated sadness" and to prepare visitors for the classical art exhibited in the Expo's Great Hall (now housing the Exploratorium ► 32). Far from making one sad, however, the palace is mysterious and enchanting, an effect greatly aided by the building's reflection in the reposeful, duck- and turtle-filled lagoon that lies alongside.

DID YOU KNOW?

- Architect: Bernard Maybeck
- Built: 1915
- Inspirations: Böcklin's *Isle of the Dead*; the drawings of Piranesi
- Materials: originally plaster and wood on a chicken-wire frame
- Height of rotunda: 132ft (40m)
- Restoration begun: 1962
- Restoration completed: 1975
- Original cost: $400,000

INFORMATION

- ✚ G3–G4; Locator map C1
- ✉ 3601 Lyon Street
- 🕐 Always open
- 🚌 28, 30
- ♿ None
- 💲 Free
- ↔ Exploratorium (► 32), Marina Green (► 58)
- ❓ City Guides (☎ 415/557–4266); free walking tour, usually twice monthly

Mission Dolores

Evidence of the 18th-century Spanish settlement of California rarely surfaces in today's San Francisco, but Mission Dolores, the oldest intact building in the city, provides a welcome, if modest, insight into the era.

California's missions Completed in 1791, the mission was the sixth in a chain of 21 built by the Spanish across California. From San Diego in the south to Sonoma in the north, each mission was located a day's horse ride from the next. The Spaniards' intention was to convert Native Americans to Catholicism, to utilize their labor and to earn their support in any colonial conflict. Mexico's independence from Spain in 1821 put the sparsely populated California in Mexican hands, and resulted in the decline and secularization of many of the missions. Most were restored under US rule, many through a job-creation program that was implemented in the 1930s during the Depression.

Inside the mission Passing through the thick adobe walls, largely responsible for the mission's success in withstanding numerous earthquakes, you first enter the small and richly atmospheric chapel, which holds an altar dating from 1780 and is decorated with frescoes executed by Native Americans. A modest assortment of historic pieces is gathered in the mission's museum, the oldest being a baptismal register for 1776. In the mission's cemetery, headstones mark Spanish- and Mexican-era notables, while the Lourdes Grotto indicates the common grave of some 5,000 Native Americans—many of whom were killed by diseases brought by the colonists. A door from the mission leads into the grandiose parish church, raised in 1918 and designated a basilica by the Pope in 1952.

Fort Mason Center

It is typical of San Francisco that the bleak exteriors of a set of former army barracks on the city's northern waterfront now hold more than 50 diverse arts centers, theaters, galleries and small museums.

Arms to art From the time of San Francisco's 18th-century Spanish *presidio* (or garrison) to the Korean War of the 1950s, Fort Mason served a military role. From 1972, however, the troop barracks were steadily transformed into a vibrant cultural center that still continues to expand.

Museums The center's museums with their temporary exhibitions include the Museo Italo-Americano, focusing on Italian-American topics, and the San Francisco Craft and Folk Art Museum where exhibitions explore many diverse avenues of artistic endeavor from the Americas and beyond. These have featured Christmas crèches, pottery from New Mexico and the acclaimed turned wooden bowls of Berkeley-based artist Bob Stocksdale. Visual arts are strongly represented in a selection of galleries, including the San Francisco Museum of Modern Art Rental Gallery, student works displayed at the Campus Coffee Gallery, and the photography, painting and sculpture liable to be on show at other spaces around the center.

HIGHLIGHTS

- San Francisco Craft and Folk Art Museum
- African-American Historical and Cultural Center
- Museo Italo-Americano
- Magic Theater
- Greens Restaurant
- Book Bay
- San Francisco Museum of Modern Art Rental Gallery
- Cowell Theater

INFORMATION

www.fortmason.org

✚ H3–J3; Locator map D1

✉ Marina Boulevard at Laguna Street

☎ 415/441–3400

🕓 Individual museums vary

🍴 Greens vegetarian restaurant

🚌 22, 28, 30, 49

♿ Few

🎟 Individual museums free or inexpensive

🔗 Golden Gate National Recreation Area (► 26), Hyde Street Pier Historical Ships (► 39), National Maritime Museum (► 55), Ghirardelli Square (► 56), Octagon House (► 57)

❓ Numerous special events

The San Francisco Craft and Folk Art Museum

35

St. Mary's Cathedral

DID YOU KNOW?

- Architects: MacSweeney, Ryan and Lee
- Design consultants: Pietro Belluschi, Pier Luigi Nervi
- Year commenced: 1960
- Year completed: 1971
- Capacity: 3,900 (2,400 seated)
- Height (including cross): 266ft (81m)
- Window dimensions: 6ft (2m) wide by 139ft (42m) tall

INFORMATION

- ✚ J5–J6; Locator map D2
- ✉ 1111 Gough Street
- ☎ 415/567-2020
- ⏰ Daily 6.30–5.30
- 🚌 2, 3, 4, 38
- ♿ Excellent
- 🆓 Free
- ➡ City Hall (➤ 37), Lafayette Park (➤ 58)

You may see the striking modern architecture of St. Mary's Cathedral on many occasions before realizing what you are looking at—its towering, gleaming white hyperbolic paraboloids are distinctly visible from across a wide section of the city. A closer inspection should not be missed.

Undivided worship The paraboloids give the cathedral a 190-ft (58-m) high ceiling and form the shape of a Greek cross. Inside, the open-plan cathedral (formally St. Mary's Catholic Cathedral of the Assumption) can seat 2,400 people. Its design is intended to eliminate the usual divisions between a cathedral's different areas. Here, the apse, nave, transepts, baptistery and narthex are undivided beneath the tall ceiling, in the center of which is a skylight in the shape of the Cross. The four stained-glass windows that rise from floor to ceiling in each main wall represent the four elements.

Cathedrals past The cathedral could hardly provide a greater contrast with its predecessor, now known as Old St. Mary's Church, which stands in Chinatown. Old St. Mary's opened as the first Catholic cathedral on the West Coast and served the city until 1891. In that year, a new St. Mary's took on the role until 1962, when it was destroyed by fire. Curiously, the present cathedral stands on a plot of land previously occupied by a supermarket, demolished to make way for the modernistic religious edifice.

The striking interior of St. Mary's Cathedral

City Hall

The crowning glory of the Civic Center complex, City Hall is a beaux-arts masterpiece with a dome that can be seen from many points around San Francisco. The esthetic appeal makes it seem an entirely fitting place for San Francisco to conduct its day-to-day administrative affairs.

A symbol City Hall's immense rotunda is topped by a black and gold copper dome (possibly modeled on St. Peter's in Rome) visible across much of the city. This intricate and inspiring building at the heart of San Francisco was completed in 1915, and arose from the drawing-boards of architects Arthur Brown and John Bakewell. Both architects studied at the École des Beaux Arts in Paris at a time when the classically inspired City Beautiful movement, which began in the 1890s, was greatly influencing American urban planning. In San Francisco, the authorities were eager for a building to symbolize San Francisco's superiority over fast-growing Los Angeles. It was Brown and Bakewell's plan—based on the French baroque style, making free use of marble and with hardly a square inch (6.5sq cm) left bare of some form of decoration—that won the day.

Interior Go inside and climb the grand staircase, lined by ornate wrought iron banisters and illuminated by freestanding and hanging lamps, and wander around the landings where porticoes and arches, topped by neoclassical sculptured guardians, give access to the upper levels. With the removal of the county courts, the building gained space as well as strength after a four-year, $300-million structural refit completed in January 1999.

DID YOU KNOW?

- Architects: Brown and Bakewell
- Prize for winning design competition: $25,000
- Building cost: $3.5 million
- Year completed: 1915
- Height of dome: 300ft (91m)
- Occupants: mayor, elected for four-year term, and Board of Supervisors, the 11-member city legislature
- Assassination: Mayor George Moscone and Supervisor Harvey Milk, 1978
- Weddings: many, including in 1980 that of Mayor Dianne Feinstein, who invited the entire city
- Previous land use: cemetery

INFORMATION

- ✚ J6; Locator map E2
- ✉ 400 Van Ness Avenue
- ☎ 415/554-4000
- 🕐 Mon–Fri 8–8
- Ⓒ Civic Center or Van Ness
- 🚌 5, 10, 20, 21, 42, 47, 49, 60, 70, 80
- ♿ Good
- 🎟 Free
- ↔ St. Mary's Cathedral (➤ 36), Asian Art Museum (➤ 40), Levi Strauss Factory (➤ 57)
- ℹ Tours: Tue–Fri 10, noon, 2, Sat–Sun 12.30

Alcatraz

DID YOU KNOW?

- Named: Isla de los Alcatraces (Island of Pelicans), 1775
- Island size: 22.5 acres (9ha)
- Number of prisoners: 1,576
- Number of cells: 450

INFORMATION

- ✚ J1; Locator map off E1
- ✉ San Francisco Bay
- ☎ 415/705–5555
- ⊙ Daily, according to first and last ferries
- 🚢 Blue & Gold Fleet from Pier 41, Fisherman's Wharf
- ♿ Few
- 💲 Expensive. Advance reservations advised in summer
- ❓ Self-guiding audio tours recommended (moderate)

This cell in Alcatraz was featured in the movie Escape from Alcatraz

Easily viewed from any high vantage point in the city, Alcatraz is as much a part of San Francisco as the Golden Gate Bridge or cable cars. The former prison sits on Alcatraz island in San Francisco Bay and is far and away the city's most chilling sight—yet one that nobody should miss.

No escape Alcatraz became the country's most feared place of incarceration from 1934, after the federal government took control of the island. It was turned into a top-security penitentiary for "incorrigible" criminals (those deemed beyond salvation and considered too dangerous to be held at conventional jails). There was one guard for every three inmates, work was a privilege that had to be earned through good behavior, and prisoners who did escape were faced with the prospect of crossing the freezing, swiftly moving waters of the bay (regarded as unswimmable) to freedom. Known escape attempts number 36; five escapees are unaccounted for and can perhaps be classed as successful.

Moody viewing The former cells, mess hall, hospital and exercise yard are all open for viewing, and an audio-cassette tour with a terse commentary by former Alcatraz guards and inmates makes an excellent atmospheric accompaniment. The costs and difficulties of running an island prison, and public disquiet at the severity of the regime, contributed to Alcatraz's closure in 1963. A small museum traces the broader history of the island, which was claimed and occupied by Native Americans in 1964 for two years under an 1868 treaty that granted them rights to "unused government land."

Hyde Street Pier Historical Ships

San Francisco was long the hub of the West Coast's maritime trade, and the vessels docked at Hyde Street Pier, as part of the National Maritime Museum, provide a reminder of the city's seafaring heyday and its dependence on waterborne travel before the building of its two bridges.

Cape Horn veteran The grandest of the ships is the *Balclutha*, a steel-hulled, square-rigged ship launched in Scotland in 1886. This vessel, originally intended to carry grain between California and Europe, rounded Cape Horn several times before ending its days transporting Alaskan salmon along the West Coast. Clamber down the ladders and around the decks for a look at the restored cabins, including the elegant saloon enjoyed by the ship's master, and to scrutinize the informative explanatory texts.

Boats of the bay The 1940s cars and trucks on the lower decks of the *Eureka* suggest the era when the vessel was the world's largest passenger ferry and able to haul more than 2,000 people and 100 vehicles between San Francisco and Sausalito in a single trip. The other exhibits are the *C. A. Thayer*, built in 1895 to move the lumber used in the construction of many early Californian cities; a 1907 deep-water steam tug, *Hercules*; *The Wapama*, built in 1915 and the last survivor of 235 Californian steam schooners; a paddle tug dating from 1914, *Eppleton Hall*, which spent its working life towing coal ships and barges in Britain; and the dainty *Alma*, a scow schooner (a type of sail-powered cargo barge) whose flat bottom enabled her to navigate with ease the shallow waters on the periphery of the bay.

HIGHLIGHTS

- *Balclutha*
- *Eureka*
- *C.A. Thayer*
- *Alma*
- *Wapama*
- *Eppleton Hall*
- Maritime Bookstore

INFORMATION

- J3; Locator map E1
- Aquatic Park, Hyde Street
- 415/561–6662
- Daily 9.30–5
- 19, 32; Hyde–Powell cable car
- None
- Inexpensive
- Fort Mason Center (➤ 35), National Maritime Museum (➤ 55), Ghirardelli Square (➤ 56)
- Occasional ranger-led tours; periodic special events

Asian Art Museum

HIGHLIGHTS

- Xuande Era blue and white porcelain
- Ming Dynasty calligraphy and fan painting
- Japanese *netsuke*
- Edo-period Japanese screen paintings
- Magnin Jade Gallery
- Tibetan *thankgas* (religious paintings)
- Tibetan thigh-bone trumpet
- Tibetan three-headed Bon figure

INFORMATION

www.asianart.org

- ➕ J/K6; Locator map E2
- ✉ Old Public Library, Larkin Street, Civic Center
- ☎ 415/581–3500
- ◕ Tue–Sun 10–5 (also Thu until 9)
- ◎ Civic Center
- ▣ 5, 19, 21, 26, 42, 47
- ♿ Excellent
- 💵 Moderate; free 1st Tue of month
- ↔ City Hall (➤ 37)
- ❓ Free tours daily. Lectures, films

Something amid the wealth of treasures inside the Asian Art Museum, the largest collection of its kind in the US, is guaranteed to catch your eye, be it Chinese jade, Japanese *netsuke* or a Tibetan thigh-bone trumpet.

Brundage collection The museum originated with an immense collection of Asian artifacts assembled by the industrialist and former president of the International Olympic Committee, Avery Brundage. San Francisco, with its historic and cultural links with Asia, was chosen as the site of a museum to display the Brundage acquisitions. Since its opening in 1966, the museum has expanded its stock considerably. In Golden Gate Park for many years, the museum reopened in the city's former main library, a larger space enabling many more of its 15,000 artifacts to be displayed.

Diversity With exhibits spanning 6,000 years and diverse cultures and religions, there is a lot to be said for simply wandering through the galleries, pausing at whatever grabs your attention. The major collections are from China and include the oldest dated example of Chinese Buddhist art (AD338), and important items from the Ming Dynasty (1368–1644) and Xuande Era (1426–35).

But the smaller and less obvious items can also delight, such as the silver work, wood carvings and textiles from Bhutan, which bring a rare insight into this obscure country.

A carved pillar in the museum

Yerba Buena Gardens

An infusion of culture in the shadow of Financial District towers, Yerba Buena Gardens is the green heart of a still-evolving 87-acre (35-ha) tract that mixes museums and arts venues with office, retail and hotel spaces.

The past During the 1970s, declining manufacturing industries were encouraged to vacate the factories clustered south of Market Street. The opening of the Moscone Convention Center in 1981 became the first step in the regeneration of an under-exploited area within walking distance of the city center, with its tourists and army of white collar workers.

The present Snaking through the landscaped greenery of Yerba Buena Gardens, the Esplanade is decorated with wacky sculptures (a harried bronze businessman and a partly sunken ship among them) and passes an artificial waterfall enclosing a monument to Martin Luther King. Adjacent, the Center for the Arts was completed in the mid-1990s with a 775-seat theater, an outdoor auditorium and several galleries with exhibitions of contemporary art, sculpture and multimedia work. Across Third Street rises the landmark Museum of Modern Art (► 46). The grey block of the Metreon (► 44) forms the Garden's west side, close to which a 1916 carousel marks the approach to Zeum (► 60)

The future Joining diverse institutions such as the California Historical Society and the Cartoon Art Museum (► 55), the city's Jewish Museum and the Mexican Museum are among those with plans to open locally. Even a rare survivor from times past, St. Patrick's Church, built in 1892 for the once immense Irish population, has plans for a sumptuous new entrance courtyard.

HIGHLIGHTS

- San Francisco Museum of Modern Art
- Esplanade and Martin Luther King Memorial
- Center for the Arts
- Zeum
- Carousel
- Cartoon Art Museum
- St. Patricks Church
- Metreon

INFORMATION

www.yerbabuenaarts.org
- L5/6; Locator map E2
- Between Fourth, Mission and Howard streets
- 415/978–ARTS
- Enquire for individual attractions
- Montgomery Street or Powell Street
- 10, 12, 15, 30, 38, 45
- Excellent
- Esplanade free; various for individual attractions
- SoMa (► 53), Marriott Hotel (► 56), SBS Building (► 57)
- Regular free events

Grace Cathedral

HIGHLIGHTS

- Ghiberti doors
- Chapel of Grace
- Stained-glass windows
- Rose window
- Gobelin tapestry

INFORMATION

- K5; Locator map E1
- 1051 Taylor Street
- 415/749–6300
- Sun–Fri 7–6, Sat 8–6
- 1; California Street cable car
- Good
- Cable Car Museum (➤ 43), Old St. Mary's Church (➤ 54), Huntington Park (➤ 58)
- Free tours daily, usually before and after services. Occasional lectures; exhibitions on social issues

It would be nice to think that Grace Cathedral, located as it is on the site of a former robber-baron's Nob Hill mansion, provides some spiritual atonement for the materialist excesses that characterize the neighborhood.

Slow building When the mansion of railroad boss Charles Crocker was destroyed by the fire that followed San Francisco's 1906 earthquake, the Crocker family donated the land to the Episcopalian church. Although the cathedral's cornerstone was laid in 1910, construction did not begin until 1928, and further delays (due partly to the Depression) resulted in Grace Cathedral's consecration being postponed until 1964. Described by its main architect, Lewis P. Hobart, as "a truly American cathedral," the cathedral is in fact neo-Gothic in style, partly modeled on Notre Dame in Paris.

Through the doors The most impressive part of the exterior is a pair of gilded bronze doors from the Lorenzo Ghiberti cast that was used for the Gates of Paradise doors of the Baptistery in Florence. Inside, a 15th-century French altarpiece and an exquisite Flemish reredos can be seen in the Chapel of Grace, while the stained-glass windows depict biblical scenes and diverse achievers such as Albert Einstein and Henry Ford. The cathedral has, controversially, frequently hosted radical figures invited to speak from its pulpit.

Grace Cathedral took more than 50 years to build

Cable Car Museum

The ring of the cable car bell provides a constant reminder that you are in San Francisco, probably the only city in the world where a relatively ineffi-cient form of public transportation is adored by the entire population.

Inspired Legend has it that a horse, slipping and falling while trying to drag its load up a San Franciscan hill, inspired Andrew Smith Hallidie—a Scots-born manufacturer of wire rope who arrived in California in 1852—to invent the cable car. Wire rope had previously been used as a means of transporting materials in gold mines, but Hallidie was the first to develop the idea as a means of moving people. Besides improving transportation throughout the city, the cable car facilitated the settlement of Nob Hill. Damage caused by the 1906 earthquake and fire, and the subsequent rise of motorized transportation, soon rendered cable cars obsolete. Pressure from San Franciscans led the federal government to award National Historic Landmark status to cable cars in 1964, however, and a provision in the city's charter ensures the preservation of the three remaining lines.

Simple but effective The museum's intriguing memorabilia, including the first cable car, tell the story of the system's development. The clever engineering principle that keeps the cars running is also revealed: each one is pulled by an underground cable that never stops moving. The "gripman" on each car uses a lever to con-nect or disconnect the car to or from the cable through a slot in the road. The whirring sound, audible as you enter the museum, is the noise made by the steel cable as it is pulled over 14-ft (4.5-m) wide winding wheels, a process visible in the museum's lower level.

DID YOU KNOW?

- First cable car run: August 2, 1873
- First route: Clay Street
- Most cars in use: 600
- Most miles of track: 112 (181km)
- Current number of cars in use: 38
- Current miles of track: 11 (18km)
- Depth of cable beneath street: 18in (46cm)
- Width of cable:1.25in (3.5cm)
- Average speed of cable car: 9.5mph (15.5kph)
- Annual cable car passengers: 10.5 million

INFORMATION

www.cablecarmuseum.com
- K4; Locator map E1
- 1201 Mason Street
- 415/474–1887
- Apr–end Sep daily 10–6; Oct–end Mar 10–5
- 1, 12, 30, 45; Powell–Mason or Powell–Hyde cable car
- Few; good on lower level
- Free
- Grace Cathedral (► 42), Chinatown (► 52), Old St. Mary's Church; Tien Hou Temple (► 54), North Beach Museum; Pacific Heritage Museum (► 55), Bank of Canton (► 57), Huntington Park (► 58), Ina Coolbrith Park (► 58)

Metreon

The Metreon's "futuristic" concept promised a new era of entertainment at its 1999 opening but some found its style to be greater than its substance. But the Metreon is undoubtedly a symbol of SoMa's regeneration.

Concept After several years of operation, this major landmark has yet to fully convince San Franciscans of its worth. It was intended to fuse with the evolving 21st-century urban landscape of Yerba Buena Gardens (► 41). The Sony-built Metreon rises five stories high and within its glass walls fills 350,000sq ft (32,550sq m) with movie theaters, stores, an eclectic mix of restaurants and state-of-the-art attractions. Within Portal 1 are interactive games such as Hyperbowl, where gamers can bowl down the streets of San Francisco, through the trees of Yosemite National Park, and across the deck of a rocking pirate ship. Or try your hand (or feet) at Dance Dance Revolution, which brings the karaoke concept to dancing.

Movies and stores Among the Metreon's 16 cinemas is a giant-screen IMAX theater—the largest in the world—using 70mm film to create ultra-realistic effects, which is also equipped to show 3D movies to headset-wearing viewers. The other theaters, equipped with ultra-comfortable seats as well the latest in projection and digital sound technology, show first-run movies. Among the shops, Sony Style reveals the latest lines in PCs, giant-screen TVs and all manner of gadgetry. Playstation offers not only the chance to try out Sony's latest games but to quiz the staff for tips and tricks on playing those you already have. Refreshingly non-globalized San Francisco-based retailers occupy the Metreon Marketplace.

DID YOU KNOW?

- Architects: Simon Martin-Vegue Winkelstein Moris; Gary Edward Handel and Associates
- Concrete: 9,000cu yd (6,885cu m)
- Steel: 65,000sq ft (6,045sq m)
- Cinema seats: 3,900
- IMAX screen: 80ft by 100ft (24m by 30m)
- Annual estimated visitors: 5 million

INFORMATION

www.metreon.com

L5; Locator map E2

4th and Mission streets

415/369–6000 or 800/METREON

Daily 10–10; individual attractions, restaurants and stores may have different openings times

Several restaurants and snack bars

Powell Street

14, 30, 45, 71

Excellent

Center free; attractions and movie theaters moderate

Yerba Buena Gardens (► 41), San Francisco Museum of Modern Art (► 46), SoMa (► 53), Cartoon Art Museum (► 55), Marriott Hotel (► 56)

Chinese Historical Society of America

The Chinese have been present for longer, and in much greater numbers, than any other non-Anglo ethnic group in San Francisco, greatly contributing to the city's multi-cultural character.

Early days The Chinese arrived in California in force during the Gold Rush, but met racial hostility and the foreign miners tax (ostensibly due from all non-US miners, but in practice only levied against the Chinese). They were unjustly blamed for the economic depression that followed the gold boom and were eventually forced into "Chinatown" communities, the largest being in San Francisco. Chinatown became populated almost exclusively by males who wore traditional dress and tied their hair in braids. Developing into the city's most densely populated districts, Chinatown was composed of wooden buildings divided by slender alleyways where, denied the comforts of traditional family life, many Chinese men gambled, smoked opium, joined the secret Chinese-American societies known as Tongs and visited prostitutes to alleviate the boredom—activities that added to the area's mystique.

Recent times Not until the founding of the Chinese Republic in 1911 were the Chinese able to adopt Western ideas and modes of dress. By the 1920s, the restaurants and shops of Chinatown were becoming tourist attractions and the Chinese, expanded in numbers through the easing of immigration restrictions, steadily became an accepted part of life. This tiny museum well documents the story of the Chinese in California, with many revealing texts alongside exhibits that range from gold-mining paraphernalia and religious objects to a 19th-century opium pipe.

DID YOU KNOW?

- Chinese in California in 1852: 25,000
- Chinese employed on transcontinental railroad in late 1860s: 10,000
- Proportion of factory jobs held by Chinese in San Francisco in 1872: 50 percent
- Chinese in San Francisco in 1875: 35,000
- Chinese in San Francisco in 1882: 26,000
- Number of Chinatown opium dens in 1885: 26
- Chinese in San Francisco in 1900: 14,000
- Chinese arrivals to San Francisco, 1910–1940: 175,000
- Estimated Chinese-Americans in San Francisco in 1990: 128,000

INFORMATION

- ✚ K4; Locator map E1
- ✉ 965 Clay Street
- ☎ 415/391–1188
- 🕐 Tue–Fri noon–5, Sat–Sun noon–4
- 🚌 1, 15, 30, 41
- ♿ None
- 💲 Free
- ↔ Transamerica Pyramid (➤ 47), Chinatown (➤ 52), Tien Hou Temple (➤ 54), North Beach Museum; Pacific Heritage Museum (➤ 55), Bank of Canton (➤ 57), Waverly Place (➤ 62)

San Francisco Museum of Modern Art

HIGHLIGHTS

- *Woman with the Hat*, Matisse
- *Head in Three-quarter View*, Picasso
- *The Coffee Pot*, Picasso
- *Guardians of the Secret*, Pollock
- *Violin and Candlestick*, Braque
- Paul Klee drawings
- Charles and Ray Eames office furniture
- *The Flower Carrier*, Rivera
- Clyfford Still gallery
- East European photography

INFORMATION

www.sfmoma.org
- L5; Locator map E2
- 151 3rd Street
- 415/357-4000
- Sun–Tue, Thu–Sat 11–6 (also Thu until 9)
- Good café
- 12, 15, 30, 45, 76
- Excellent
- Moderate; free 1st Tue of month
- Yerba Buena Gardens (► 41), SoMa (► 53), Cartoon Art Museum (► 55), Marriott Hotel (► 56), SBS Building (► 57)
- Free tours daily. Lectures, films, other events

Striking and sympathetic architecture, outstanding collections that span painting, sculpture, drawing, photography and furniture, and innovative temporary exhibitions, make SFMOMA a showplace befitting a forward-thinking city.

Main attraction The core of the museum's permanent collections highlights painting and sculpture from 1900 to 1970. Among significant contributions from Europeans are Pablo Picasso's *Head in Three-quarter View* and *The Coffee Pot*, and Georges Braque's *Violin and Candlestick*. Do not miss the museum's prize possession: Matisse's *Woman with the Hat*, painted in 1905; a work that made a crucial contribution to what became the century's first radical art movement—fauvism. A striking complement of abstract expressionist canvases includes Jackson Pollock's *Guardians of the Secret*, contributions from Willem de Kooning, and the last work by color-field painter Barnett Newman. Latin-American artists are also given prominent space; among the best are the intriguing Mexican modernists Diego Rivera and Frida Kahlo.

Other galleries With 17,000 exhibits spread across six floors and over 200,000sq ft (18,600sq m), the museum has much space to devote to California art. The canvases of Richard Diebenkorn have particular impact and relevance to the region, as do the 28 works donated by California-based abstract expressionist Clyfford Still. The Phyllis Wattis Theater (main floor) features film screenings, artist lectures and other presentations. The museum is also equipped to stage provocative exhibitions in the emerging fields of video, computer and interactive art.

Transamerica Pyramid

The Transamerica Pyramid is San Francisco's most distinctive building and arguably the most innovative modern contribution to the city's skyline. Stepping inside is hard to resist, although doing so may prove to be somewhat anticlimactic.

Perfect profile   San Franciscans were slow to appreciate the splendor of the 853-ft (260-m) high building's unique profile, rising above the Financial District's forest of even-sided high-rises with a slowly tapering spire flanked by windowless wings, and with a decorative spire rising for 212ft (65m) above the 48th floor. Yet the Transamerica Pyramid adds greatly to the city skyline and has steadily been accepted since 1972. The owners, the Transamerica Corporation, grew from various companies built around the Bank of Italy (later renamed the Bank of America), which was established in San Francisco in 1904.

Inside   To help withstand earthquakes, the structure sits on a steel and concrete block sunk 50ft (15m) into the ground. The building is a place of work for the 1,500 employees of the 50 firms who rent its space. Cameras mounted at the top of the

pyramid are linked to monitors in the lobby, which reveal a birds-eye-view of the city (fog permitting). Since 11 September the lobby has been closed to the general public and the monitors are only visable through the north side windows.

DID YOU KNOW?

- Architect: William L. Pereira & Associates
- Smallest floor: 48th, 45ft (14m) per side
- Largest floor: 5th, 145ft (44m) per side
- Angle of slope: 5 degrees
- Depth of excavation: 52ft (16m)
- Number of floors: 48

INFORMATION

- L4; Locator map.E1
- 600 Montgomery Street
- Reasonable restaurant
- Open to employees only
- 15, 41
- Good
- Free
- Chinese Historical Society of America (➤ 45), Wells Fargo Museum (➤ 48), Chinatown (➤ 52), Old St. Mary's Church; Tien Hou Temple (➤ 54), North Beach Museum; Pacific Heritage Museum (➤ 55), Bank of America Center (➤ 56), Bank of Canton (➤ 57), Transamerica Redwood Park (➤ 58), Waverly Place (➤ 62)

Wells Fargo Museum

INFORMATION

L4–L5; Locator map E1
420 Montgomery Street
415/396–2619
Mon–Fri 9–5
1, 12, 15, 42; California Street cable car
Good
Free

The company has grown into one of the leading US financial institutions, but for many the name of Wells Fargo is synonymous with the early days of the American West, and this collection ably demonstrates the historic links.

Going west After establishing an express mail service in the east by the 1840s, Henry Wells and William G. Fargo began viewing the opportunities offered by Gold Rush-era California with relish, and they opened an office in San Francisco in 1852. Whether buying, selling, or transporting gold, transferring funds or delivering mail, the company earned a reputation for trustworthiness in an era dominated by rogues. By 1861, Wells Fargo & Co. was operating the western leg of the famed Pony Express (which ran for only 18 months) and, by the late 1860s, monopolized the movement of mail across the western United States. In 1905 the mail delivery and banking divisions of the company were separated, when the latter combined with the Nevada Bank—founded by the San Francisco-based silver barons of the Comstock Lode—setting Wells Fargo on the path to becoming a major player in the world of American high finance.

Looking back A few steps from the site of the company's 1852 office, the Wells Fargo Museum (inside the Wells Fargo Bank) entertainingly documents the rise of the company. Sitting inside an 1860s stagecoach provides one highlight, but there is much more to see amid the clutter of a re-created Gold Rush-era Wells Fargo office: gold-weighing scales, bulky mining tools, gold coins and numerous aging letters that miraculously survived their trip across the rutted tracks of the old West.

Oakland Museum of California

If you only make one crossing of San Francisco Bay, make it to Oakland where the Oakland Museum of California leads the way in documenting the extraordinary history, nature, and art of the Golden State.

Nature The remarkable plant and animal life living in the high mountains, low deserts and other habitats of California are revealed by the 38,000-sq ft (3,530-sq m) Hall of Ecology's elaborate dioramas. The adjoining Aquatic California Gallery does a similar job for underwater life, illustrating the goings-on in California's rivers, bays and hot springs, and beneath the ocean.

History Every episode in California's past is remembered here, thoughtfully explored and copiously documented. The collections are enhanced by interactive computers providing detailed information on particular exhibits, recorded commentaries from experts and oral histories. From outlining the conflicts between indigenous Californians and the colonizing Spaniards, the collections come up to date with the rise of Californian computer companies and the invention of the mountain bike.

Californian art An imaginative selection of exhibits on the top floor of the museum demonstrates how the art of California has developed from 19th-century depictions of its untamed, natural beauty, through to the self-confidence of later 20th-century Californian artists such as semi-abstract painter Richard Diebenkorn and ceramicist Peter Voulkos. The photography collection includes outstanding contributions from Dorothea Lange and Maynard Dixon, both of whom were based in San Francisco.

HIGHLIGHTS

- *Yosemite Valley*, Bierstadt
- *Migrant Mother*, Lange
- Re-created Nevada City assay office
- Re-created "beatnik" coffee house
- Ness's custom motorcycles
- *California Miner with Packhorse*, Raschen
- *San Francisco, July 1849*, Davis

INFORMATION

www.museumca.org
- Off map at N3; Locator map off F1
- 1000 Oak Street, Oakland
- 510/238-2200
- Wed–Sat 10–5, Sun noon–5 (also 1st Fri of month 10–9)
- Good café
- Lake Merritt
- Excellent
- Inexpensive; free 2nd Sun of month
- Free tours. Films, lectures, and events

U.C., Berkeley Campus

HIGHLIGHTS

- Sproul Plaza
- Sather Tower (also called the Campanile—carillon recitals on Sunday afternoons)
- Hearst Mining Building
- Phoebe A. Hearst Museum of Anthropology
- Berkeley Art Museum and the Pacific Film Archive
- Sather Gate
- Lawrence Hall of Science
- Morrison Library
- Bancroft Library

INFORMATION

www.berkeley.edu
- ✚ Off map at N3; Locator map off F1
- ✉ Main Gate, Bancroft Way
- ☎ 510/642–5215
- 🕐 Daylight hours recommended
- Ⓑ Berkeley
- ♿ Good
- 👆 Free
- ❓ Tours Mon–Sat 10, Sun 1

Children play on the DNA model on Berkeley campus

A haven of 1960s student dissent, the University of California, Berkeley campus might be less radical than it once was, but its buildings and museums and the picture it provides of contemporary student life easily justify a trip.

Past The first college at Berkeley opened in the 1850s, but a lack of funds allowed the facility to be purchased in 1873 by the state government as the first of what are now six campuses of the University of California. Much of the university's early finance came as donations from Phoebe Apperson Hearst, wife of a wealthy mining baron and mother of the even more wealthy publishing tycoon, William Randolph Hearst. In the 1940s, Robert Oppenheimer was U.C., Berkeley's professor of physics before moving to Los Alamos to work on the first atomic bomb. In 1964, the seeds of what evolved into countrywide student rebellions were sown by the sit-ins and rallies of Berkeley's Free Speech Movement.

Present U.C., Berkeley's 30,000 students are now more concerned with acquiring a good degree than immersing themselves in radical politics, though there is no shortage of causes and campaigns being promoted along Sproul Plaza, in the heart of the campus. Elsewhere around the 100-acre (40-ha) campus are museums, libraries and architecturally distinguished buildings, such as John Galen Howard's beaux arts-style Hearst Mining Building. Galen was also responsible for the elegant Sather Gate, marking the main entrance to the campus opposite Telegraph Avenue.

SAN FRANCISCO's
best

Neighborhoods

FISHERMAN'S WHARF

Directly north of North Beach is Fisherman's Wharf, the only section of San Francisco pitched squarely at visitors. Former factories and fishing piers have been carefully and imaginatively converted to complexes of stores, restaurant and tourist attractions. Despite the obvious commercial trappings, Fisherman's Wharf draws 12 million visitors each year and is, for most, a very enjoyable experience.

A street in Chinatown

CHINATOWN
The compact streets and alleyways of Chinatown's 24 history-laden blocks are home to one of the largest Asian communities outside Asia. Several 100-year-old temples, fortune-cookie factories and numerous exotic stores are crammed into one of the city's most energetic and ethnically distinct neighborhoods. The area also holds some of the city's best-value restaurants.
✚ K–L 4–5 🚌 1, 15, 30, 45, 83; California Street cable car

HAIGHT-ASHBURY
Holding hundreds of elegant Victorian homes that survived the 1906 earthquake and fire, and becoming world famous as the heart of hippiedom in 1967, Haight-Ashbury has long been the most tolerant section of a tolerant city. It has exceptional vintage clothing outlets and used-bookstores, and remains a lively center for alternative arts, culture and lifestyles despite increasing gentrification.
✚ F–H 6–8 🚌 6, 7, 24, 33, 43, 66, 71

JAPANTOWN
Japanese temples, stores and restaurants, and Japanese-style residential architecture, make this the spiritual home of San Francisco's Japanese-American population, even though comparatively few Japanese-Americans live here.
✚ H5 🚌 2, 3, 4, 22, 38

MISSION DISTRICT
With Latin-American bakeries and restaurants, and some of its streets decorated by stunning murals (➤ 61), the Mission District holds the bulk of the city's Latino population. The neighborhood's Mexican-American population, established here in the 1940s, was joined from the 1970s by arrivals from Central America's war-torn countries. From the late 1990s, the area saw protests as its traditionally low rents were raised by an influx of "dotcommers," non-San Franciscans with high-paid internet-related jobs.
✚ J–K 7–9 🚇 16th Street Mission, 24th Street Mission 🚌 12, 14, 26, 33, 49, 67

NOB HILL
A quartet of extremely wealthy Californians (the "Big Four") built the first million-dollar mansions on Nob Hill from the 1870s. The 1906 earthquake and fire destroyed all but one of the district's opulent homes, but Nob Hill's pedigree is still evident. The area holds exclusive hotels and a very well-dressed congregation shows up for Sunday services at the neighborhood's Grace Cathedral (➤ 42).
✚ K5 🚌 1, 27; California Street cable car

NORTH BEACH

North Beach's wealth of cafés and bookstores recall its links with the Beat Generation of the 1950s. Meanwhile, the abundant Italian-owned restaurants and stores are reminders of the Italians who settled in the district in force from the late 19th century.

✚ K4 ☐ 15, 30, 39, 41, 45, 83

PACIFIC HEIGHTS

You could spend hours wandering the wide streets, marveling at the opulence of Pacific Heights, which draws the wealthiest strata of San Franciscan society to its lavish Victorian mansions and high-rise luxury apartment buildings boasting wonderful views to Alcatraz and beyond.

✚ G–J 4–5 ☐ 1, 3, 22, 24, 41, 42, 45, 47, 49

RUSSIAN HILL

A noted bohemian enclave in the late 19th century, Russian Hill is still a home of writers and artists, though only those with established reputations—and commensurate incomes—can afford to live among the successful doctors and lawyers of today.

✚ J–K 3–4 ☐ 41, 45; Powell–Hyde cable car

SOMA

Many of the former warehouses and factories of SoMa, an abbreviation of "South of Market Street," have been transformed into nightclubs, restaurants and the offices of internet and multimedia companies. The biggest boost has been the development of the 12-block Yerba Buena Gardens (▶ 41), a cultural complex with galleries, museums, performance venues, a bowling alley, green spaces and landscaped walkways.

✚ J–M 5–7 ☐ 10, 12, 14, 15, 20, 26, 27, 30, 45, 50, 60, 70, 76, 80

Victorian houses near Russian Hill

THE CASTRO

The rainbow flags of gay solidarity are a common sight above the streets of the Castro, west of the Mission District, settled in large numbers by gay men (and by lesser numbers of lesbians) from the 1970s. As gays campaigned for and won a voice in city politics, the Castro evolved into the world's largest and most famous gay neighborhood.

HAYES VALLEY

Immediately west of Civic Center on and around Hayes Street (between Franklin and Octavia streets) is an increasingly trendy grouping of stores, art galleries, bars and restaurants, collectively known as Hayes Valley.

Places of Worship

CHURCH OF STS. PETER AND PAUL

Long the major place of worship for North Beach's Italian community, this imposing Romanesque edifice was founded in 1922. The twin spires rise above Washington Square and are evocatively illuminated at night.

✚ K4 ✉ 666 Filbert Street ☎ 415/421–0809 🕐 Usually 7.30am–8pm 🚌 15, 30, 39, 41, 45 ✋ Free

OLD ST. MARY'S CHURCH

The West Coast's first Catholic cathedral and a forerunner of today's ultramodern St. Mary's Cathedral (► 36), Old St. Mary's was completed in 1854.

✚ K5 ✉ 660 California Street ☎ 415/288–3840 🕐 Mon–Fri, Sun 7–3.30, Sat 11–6 🚌 1, 15; California Street cable car ✋ Free

ST. JOHN COLTRANE AFRICAN ORTHODOX CHURCH

Almost certainly the most curious church in San Francisco (see panel for details).

✚ H7 ✉ 930 Gough Street ☎ 415/673–3572 🕐 Service: Sun from noon 🚌 24

SWEDENBORGIAN CHURCH

In keeping with Swedenborgian beliefs, this diminutive church resembles a finely crafted log cabin. Completed in 1895, the church was the work of several leading figures of the California Arts and Crafts movement.

✚ G5 ✉ 2107 Lyon Street ☎ 415/346–6466 🕐 Mon–Fri 9–5 🚌 3, 43 ✋ Free

TEMPLE EMANU-EL

This immense Byzantine-style structure, able to seat 2,000 people, looms above the surrounding residential architecture. Finished in 1926 at a cost of $3 million, the temple was raised to serve the longest-established Jewish congregation in California.

✚ F5 ✉ Lake Street and Arguello Boulevard ☎ 415/751–2535 🕐 Guided tours only Mon–Fri 1–3 🚌 1, 4, 33 ✋ Free

TIEN HOU TEMPLE

Dating from 1852, this is the oldest and most atmospheric of Chinatown's incense-charged temples. Offerings of fruit, commonly oranges or tangerines, are placed before the altar by believers.

✚ K4 ✉ 4th floor, 125 Waverly Place 🕐 Erratic, but usually Mon–Sat 10.30–4 🚌 1, 15, 30, 45, 83 ✋ Donation

Old St. Mary's Church

ST. JOHN COLTRANE AFRICAN ORTHODOX CHURCH

St. John Coltrane African Orthodox Church was founded in 1971 by a jazz fan who underwent a religious experience when hearing saxophonist John Coltrane play live in the 1960s. The fan is now a sax-playing bishop who leads a congregation that is encouraged to bring instruments and to play them during the services.

Museums

A SUBMARINE TOUR

After touring the National Maritime Museum, continue the nautical theme by exploring the claustrophobic innards of USS *Pampanito*, moored a few minutes' walk away at Pier 45. Launched in 1943, the submarine saw action in the Pacific and sank 27,000 tons of enemy shipping. The cramped crews' and officers' quarters, the engine rooms and the torpedo room are included on a self-guided tour.

CARTOON ART MUSEUM

Be they from comics, TV, or the movies—or culled from the deepest recesses of history—cartoons are accorded the seriousness of art in the changing exhibitions staged here, these seldom failing to be thought-provoking and entertaining. Displays cover artists from Hanna-Barbera to Charlie Brown.

🔲 K6 ✉ 655 Mission Street ☎ 415/227–8666 🕐 Tue–Sun 11–5
🚌 Any Market Street bus 💵 Moderate

MARITIME MUSEUM

A fine collection of figureheads, model ships and other nautical memorabilia recalls San Francisco's seafaring and shipbuilding past. The building itself resembles an ocean liner and provides a fine example of the 1930s art-deco Streamline Moderne style.

🔲 J3 ✉ Aquatic Park, foot of Polk Street
☎ 415/561–7100 🕐 Daily 10–5 🚌 19, 32;
Powell–Hyde cable car 💵 Free

NORTH BEACH MUSEUM

Temporary exhibitions of photographs and paraphernalia document various episodes in the eventful past of this distinctive neighborhood.

🔲 K4 ✉ Mezzanine level, 1435 Stockton Street
☎ 415/391–6210 🕐 Mon–Fri 9–5 🚌 30, 45
💵 Free

PACIFIC HERITAGE MUSEUM

Underrated ever-changing collection that focuses on the arts, culture and economies of the Pacific-Asia region, often highlighting San Francisco's role in the area. Situated on the edge of Chinatown, the museum is run by the United Commercial Bank and occupies the site of the 1875 US Sub-Treasury, which is also detailed by the exhibits.

🔲 L4 ✉ 608 Commercial Street ☎ 415/362–4100 🕐 Tue–Sat
10–4 🚌 1, 15, 30, 41 💵 Free

Moebius's The Major, *in the Cartoon Art Museum*

Modern Buildings

ART AND ARCHITECTURE

Besides holding an excellent art collection, the San Francisco Museum of Modern Art (► 46) is also a distinguished architectural addition to the city. Opened in 1995, the $60-million museum was designed by Swiss architect Mario Botta, who gave it a stepped-back brick and stone façade. A truncated cylinder rising through the center allows light to flood the interior's full-height atrium.

BANK OF AMERICA CENTER
No longer owned by the bank whose name it bears but still a supreme example of inspired 1960s' high-rise office architecture. The 52-story building's dark red exterior, dominating the area by day, seems to become almost transparent at sunset.
➕ L5 ✉ 555 California Street 🚍 15, 42; California Street cable car

101 CALIFORNIA STREET
This Philip Johnson/John Burgee office tower is a soaring glass-sided silo that masquerades as a greenhouse at street level.
➕ L5 ✉ 101 California Street 🚍 California Street cable car

GHIRARDELLI SQUARE
One of Fisherman's Wharf's successful conversions, the red-brick shell of the chocolate factory that opened here in 1893 now holds a strollable complex of shops and restaurants.
➕ J3 ✉ 900 North Point Street 🚍 19, 42; Powell–Hyde cable car

140 MAIDEN LANE
During the late 1940s, architect Frank Lloyd Wright undertook a complete remodeling of this 1911 building and the design provided a foretaste of his acclaimed Guggenheim Museum in New York. The exterior brickwork is imbued with Mayan motifs; go inside to find the distinctive spiral ramp.
➕ K5 ✉ 140 Maiden Lane 🚍 2, 3, 4, 30, 45

MARRIOTT HOTEL
A voluminous 40-story structure, the largest building in the city, the hotel sharply divided opinion when it opened in 1989. Newspaper columnist Herb Caen derisively dubbed it the "jukebox Marriott."
➕ L5 ✉ 777 Market Street 🚍 5, 6, 7, 8, 9, 21, 31, 38

RINCON CENTER
An office and shopping complex grafted with great style onto the rear of a 1930s art-deco post office. The latter retains a vibrant 1939 mural depicting scenes from California's history.
➕ L5–M5 ✉ Mission Street, between Spear and Steuart streets 🚍 14

The ultramodern architecture of the Rincon Center is complemented by this decorative stylus

Historic Buildings

BANK OF CANTON
A three-tiered, pagoda-style structure erected in 1909 as the Chinatown telephone exchange; it was converted into a bank in the 1950s.
➕ K4 ✉ 743 Washington Street 🚌 1, 15, 30, 45

FERRY BUILDING
Completed in 1903, the 235-ft (71-m) high Ferry Building was for many years the city's tallest structure. Surviving the 1906 earthquake and fire—and a plan to demolish it for safety reasons during the disaster—the slender tower became a symbol of San Francisco's ability to survive natural catastrophe.
➕ M4 ✉ Foot of Market Street 🚌 5, 6, 7, 8, 9, 21, 31

HAAS-LILIENTHAL HOUSE
This elaborate 1886 example of the Queen Anne style of architecture is also the only San Franciscan Victorian building to retain its period-furnished rooms.
➕ J4 ✉ 2007 Franklin Street ☎ 415/441–3000 🕐 Guided tours Wed, Sat noon–3, Sun 11–4 🚌 83 💵 Inexpensive

LEVI STRAUSS FACTORY
Built by Levi Strauss after the 1906 earthquake and still producing the world-famous jeans.
➕ J7 ✉ 250 Valencia Street ☎ 415/565–9153 🚌 26

OCTAGON HOUSE
One of five eight-sided houses in San Francisco (only two of which still stand ► 62), their shape considered lucky by the owners. The Octagon House dates from 1861 and the restoration program was organized by the Colonial Dames of America whose exhibitions of Colonial- and Federal-period arts and crafts now fill the interior.
➕ H4 ✉ 2645 Gough Street 🚌 41, 45

SBC BUILDING
A stylish skyscraper of the 1920s, its design heavily influenced by the work of Eliel Saarinen.
➕ L5 ✉ 140 New Montgomery Street 🚌 5, 6, 7, 8, 9, 15, 21, 30, 31, 38, 45, 71

VEDANTA TEMPLE
An extraordinary conglomeration of turquoise-colored towers, turrets and domes, built in 1905 for an orthodox Hindu sect.
➕ H4 ✉ 2963 Webster Street 🚌 22, 41, 45

Octagon House

LEVI'S JEANS
German-born entrepreneur Levi Strauss arrived in San Francisco in 1853 and began manufacture of what he called a "waist-high overall" for use by workers in the Californian gold mines. Hard-wearing, with tough seams, copper rivets and numerous pockets, the Strauss garments evolved into "jeans," their popularity spreading across the American West and around the world.

Green Spaces

ANGEL ISLAND STATE PARK

For a day in the wilds, make the short ferry crossing from Fisherman's Wharf to the mile-square (1.5km) Angel Island. The largest piece of land in San Francisco Bay, the island is a state park with foot trails and bicycle paths navigating its thickly forested heart. Also explorable are the remains of a military prison and of an immigration processing center.

*Washington Square,
North Beach*

HUNTINGTON PARK

Facing Grace Cathedral (➤ 42), Huntington Park occupies the plot of an 1872 mansion and is named for railroad baron Collis P. Huntington.

➕ K5 ⊠ Bordered by California, Sacramento, Taylor and Cushman streets ▤ 1; California Street cable car

INA COOLBRITH PARK

A tiny but abundantly vegetated park accessed by steps and named for the woman who, in 1919, became California's first poet laureate. Coolbrith's literary get-togethers, held at her Russian Hill home, were legendary.

➕ K4 ⊠ Bordered by Taylor and Vallejo streets ▤ Powell–Mason cable car

LAFAYETTE PARK

The highest point in Pacific Heights and overlooked by the splendid Spreckels Mansion, completed in 1912 as the home of sugar-baron Adolph Spreckels and his wife.

➕ H5–J5 ⊠ Bordered by Gough, Laguna, Sacramento and Washington streets ▤ 1, 12

MARINA GREEN

Kite flying, jogging and the walking of well-bred dogs are among the popular pursuits in this bay-side green strip, overlooked by pastel-colored stucco-fronted houses and serving an affluent neighborhood.

➕ G3–H3 ⊠ Beside Marina Boulevard ▤ 22

TRANSAMERICA REDWOOD PARK

Located behind the Transamerica Pyramid (➤ 47) and a welcome break from the hubbub of the Financial District, this slender park holds young redwood trees and stages free lunchtime concerts on weekdays.

➕ L4 ⊠ Bordered by Washington and Clay streets ▤ 15, 41

WASHINGTON SQUARE

Packed each morning with Chinese going through their t'ai chi routines, this North Beach park is also the scene for enjoyable art shows each weekend.

➕ K4 ⊠ Bordered by Columbus Avenue and Filbert, Union and Stockton streets ▤ 15, 30, 39, 41, 45

Views

ALAMO SQUARE

Perhaps the most photographed view in San Francisco finds the six Victorian homes, or "painted ladies," on the east side of Alamo Square contrasting with the modern towers of the Financial District visible in the background.

➕ H6 ☒ Bordered by Hayes, Fulton, Scott and Steiner streets 🚌 21

COIT TOWER

Whether from the top of the tower or from its base, the view across San Francisco Bay and a huge swath of the city is a memorable one, as are the murals—part of a Depression-era project to give work to artists.

➕ K3 ☒ Summit of Telegraph Hill Boulevard 🚌 39

FAIRMONT HOTEL CROWN ROOM ELEVATOR

The glass-sided elevator that rises nonstop to the 22nd-floor Crown Room restaurant brings vertiginous views of the Financial District as it recedes far below.

➕ K5 ☒ 950 Mason Street 🚌 1; California Street cable car

SUTRO HEIGHTS PARK

From the former grounds of the home of legendary 19th-century San Francisco benefactor Adolph Sutro are fabulous views of the city's Pacific coast and the western end of Golden Gate Park. Remnants of the house and its statuary are scattered about the park.

➕ A6 ☒ Bordered by Point Lobos Avenue, Great Highway and 48th Street 🚌 18, 38

TWIN PEAKS

One of the best overall views of San Francisco comes, not surprisingly, from one of its highest points, the 913-ft (278-m) summit of the two hills known as Twin Peaks; even on foot, the exhausting ascent is worthwhile.

➕ G9 ☒ Summit of Twin Peaks Boulevard 🚌 37

*The view from
Twin Peaks*

MARIN HEADLANDS

If the view of San Francisco from the Marin Headlands looks strangely familiar that's because it has been the subject of countless photos, films and videos: the city appearing through the cables of the Golden Gate Bridge, which looms large in the foreground. Fear not if your trip is made on a foggy day: A moody shroud around the towers of the bridge make for a great San Francisco snap. Part of Golden Gate National Recreation Area (➤ 26).

Marin Headlands Visitor Center ☎ 415/331–1540
🕐 9.30–4.30

For Kids

BEACHES
China and Baker beaches, which are part of Golden Gate National Recreation Area (► 26), make appealing locations for enjoying a picnic and a frolic in the sand.

Few can resist a ride on a cable car

CABLE CAR RIDE
Any cable car is an enjoyable adventure for most children, but to avoid the lines at the main embarkation points take the California Street line.
✉ Operate on three routes (► 7) ☎ General public transportation information 415/673–MUNI ⏰ Daily 6.30am–12.30am 💷 Inexpensive

CALIFORNIA ACADEMY OF SCIENCES
The wonders of ants, astrobiology, the coral reef and the mysterious creatures of the deep are among the subjects innovatively tackled at this place of fun and learning, housed here for a few years as its Golden Gate Park home is rebuilt. Founded in 1853 by a small group of enthusiasts who held weekly meetings and published papers on the state's newly discovered animal species, the California Academy of Sciences has evolved into a sizable museum.
✚ L6 ✉ 875 Howard Street ☎ 415/321–8000 ⏰ Daily 10–5 Ⓠ Powell Street 🚌 2, 3, 4, 5, 6, 7, 9, 12, 14, 21, 30, 31, 38, 45, 66, 71 💷 Moderate

SAN FRANCISCO ZOO
Awkwardly located on the fringes of the city, this zoo nevertheless holds the usual complement of creatures, plus a state-of-the-art primate center and a Children's Zoo where furry creatures aplenty can be stroked.
✚ Off map at B10 ✉ Sloat Boulevard and 45th Avenue ☎ 415/753–7080 ⏰ Daily 10–5 🚌 18, 23; L 💷 Moderate

ZEUM
Part of the Rooftop complex, which also includes a skating rink and bowling alley, above the Moscone Convention Center, Zeum is an ingeniously designed high-tech media center for kids, allowing participants to make video and sound recordings, and lots more, using the most up-to-date technology.
✚ L6 ✉ Corner of Howard and 4th streets ☎ 415/777–2800 ⏰ Wed–Sun 11–5 🚌 30, 76 Ⓠ Powell Street ♿ Excellent 💷 Moderate

PIER 39'S SEA LIONS
Introducing young minds to the wonders of natural California can easily be accomplished at Fisherman's Wharf's Pier 39. Attracted by an abundant supply of herring, some 600 California sea lions have made their homes beside the pier and can be observed from a marked viewing area. A naturalist arrives between 11 and 5 to talk about the creatures most weekends (for details ☎ 415/705–5500).

What's Free

CHINESE CULTURAL CENTER

On the third floor of the towering Holiday Inn—which looms above Portsmouth Square and its legions of elderly Chinese men indulging in games of chance—are rotating exhibitions that explore diverse aspects of Chinese culture and artistic traditions.
➕ L4 ✉️ Holiday Inn, 750 Kearny Street ☎️ 415/986–1822
🕐 Tue–Sat 10–4 🚌 15

DIEGO RIVERA GALLERY

An immense mural by the Mexican master, Diego Rivera sits at one end of this gallery of the highly respected San Francisco Institute of Art, while student works line the other three walls.
➕ J3 ✉️ 800 Chestnut Street ☎️ 415/771–7020 🕐 Daily 9–9
🚌 15, 30, 41; Powell–Hyde cable car

FORT POINT NATIONAL HISTORIC SITE

Completed in 1861, Fort Point was intended to deter enemy incursions into San Francisco Bay during the Civil War and World War II but never a shot was fired in anger. Period-attired guides describe the fort's past; temporary indoor exhibitions explore aspects of US military history.
➕ D3 ✉️ Beneath Golden Gate Bridge ☎️ 415/556–1693
🕐 Fri–Sun 10–5 🚌 28, 29, 76

MISSION DISTRICT MURALS

Some of the best of the Mission District's many murals, reflecting Latin-American muralist traditions, line this alley and focus on a theme of peace in Central America. Visit during daylight hours.
➕ K9 ✉️ Balmy Alley, between 24th and 25th streets
☎️ 415/285–2287 (Precita Eyes Mural Center) 🚌 12, 27, 67

NATIONAL JAPANESE AMERICAN HISTORICAL SOCIETY

In the heart of Japantown, these changing exhibitions document varied aspects of the Japanese-American life over several generations, including the community's contribution to sport, the military, dining and the legacy of unfair internment during World War II.
➕ H5 ✉️ 1684 Post Street ☎️ 415/431–5007 🕐 Telephone for schedule 🚌 2, 3, 4, 76

HOTEL ART

Public areas in San Franciscan hotels can prove rewarding for art and photography enthusiasts: The Palace (➤ 86) has an excellent Maxfield Parrish mural and the Compass Rose Room at the Westin St. Francis (➤ 86) holds photographs by Ansel Adams.

African-American mural in the Mission District

Intriguing Streets

CHESTNUT STREET
A mix of shops, eateries and bars have given this Marina District thoroughfare an effervescent mood and a strong reputation as a haunt of the young, affluent and unattached.
➕ G/H4 ✉ Between Divisadero and Fillmore streets 🚌 30

GREEN STREET
Among the numerous architecturally distinguished survivors of the 1906 earthquake and fire along this single block is the Feusier Octagon House, number 1067, one of the city's two remaining eight-sided homes (➤ 57).
➕ J4–K4 ✉ Between Jones and Leavenworth streets 🚌 41, 45; Powell–Hyde cable car

LOMBARD STREET
Traffic zigzags very slowly down Lombard Street, "the crookedest street in San Francisco," moving around colorful gardens put in place during the 1920s.
➕ J4 ✉ Between Hyde and Leavenworth streets 🚌 15, 19, 30

MACONDRAY LANE
With leafy trees shading its cottages, most of which were raised in the construction boom that followed the 1906 earthquake, pedestrianized Macondray Lane, the setting of Maupin's *Tales of the City*, is the epitome of quaint and cozy Russian Hill.
➕ J4–K4 ✉ Between Taylor and Leavenworth streets 🚌 41, 45; Powell–Hyde cable car

MAIDEN LANE
Notorious for its brothels in the 1800s, this road is now lined by smart stores and bordered by fancy white gates.
➕ K5–L5 ✉ Between Stockton and Kearny streets 🚌 2, 3, 4, 30, 45

UNION STREET
The affluent, fashionable residents of Pacific Heights shop, eat and socialize along these few chic blocks.
➕ H4–J4 ✉ Between Franklin and Steiner streets 🚌 22, 41, 45

WAVERLY PLACE
A Chinatown side street holding three temples, numerous Chinese family association buildings and the decorations that earn it the name "street of painted balconies."
➕ K4–K5 ✉ Between Sacramento and Washington streets 🚌 1, 15, 30, 45, 83

FILBERT STEPS

Steep gradients are a San Franciscan specialty and often cause streets to become flights of steps. One such is the Filbert Steps, running between Telegraph Hill (from Coit Tower) and Levi's Plaza. Curiously, the gardens that line Filbert Steps are the result of the horticultural enterprise of a one-time Hollywood stunt lady, who moved here on her retirement in 1949.

SAN FRANCISCO
where to

EAT

SHOP

BE ENTERTAINED

STAY

American

PRICES

Expect to pay per person excluding drink:

$ up to $15
$$ $15–$30
$$$ $30–$50
$$$$ more than $50

Except for a handful of very expensive "destination" restaurants, dining in San Francisco is a cost-effective experience. Anticipate spending $6–$8 per person for breakfast, around $10 for lunch and $15–$20 for dinner excluding drinks. Wherever you dine, a tip of at least 15 percent of the total is expected; reward extremely good service with a tip of 20 percent or more.

OPENING TIMES

Peak hours for lunch are 11.30–2 and for dinner 5.30–9, but many restaurants open earlier and/or close later than these times. All the restaurants listed are open daily for lunch and dinner unless otherwise stated.

CONTEMPORARY

BACAR ($$$)

Housed in a three level space, with live jazz, a terrific wine selection and late-night service.
➕ L6 ✉ 448 Brannan Street ☎ 415/904–4100 🚌 9, 15, 30, 45

BIX ($$$)

Tucked away on a downtown alley, this atmospheric supper club is always packed.
➕ L4 ✉ 56 Gold Street (between Jackson and Pacific streets) ☎ 415/433–6300 🚌 15, 42

BOULEVARD ($$$$)

Try to nab a seat in the back room of this Embarcadero restaurant where you can gaze at Bay Bridge as you dive into superb New American cuisine. Dishes include wild mushroom risotto, pork loin garnished with onion rings and steaks.
➕ L5 ✉ 1 Mission Street ☎ 415/543–6084 🕐 Dinner only Sat, Sun 🚌 1, 14, 41; F

DESIREE CAFE ($–$$)

What looks like a simple café inside the Presidio's San Francisco Film Center turns out to offer a low-key outlet for a noted city chef; small menu of inventive and nutritious fare with a California edge.
➕ F4 ✉ 39 Mesa Street, Suite 118 ☎ 415/561–2336 🕐 Breakfast and lunch; closed Sat and Sun 🚌 29

GARY DANKO ($$$$)

One of the city's finest restaurants, located in Russian Hill; choose from the 3–5-course tasting menu. Impeccable service.
➕ J3 ✉ 800 North Point Street ☎ 415/749–2060 🕐 Dinner only 🚌 19, 30, 42; Powell–Hyde cable car

HARRIS' ($$$–$$$$)

A haven for lovers of red meat, Harris' has a strong reputation for delivering steaks, ribs and other prime cuts to perfection, in an elegant Pacific Heights setting.
➕ J4 ✉ 2100 Van Ness Avenue ☎ 415/673–1800 🚌 12, 42, 47, 49, 76

POSTRIO ($$$$)

Run by celebrity chef Wolfgang Puck, this is the epitome of Californiam-style elegant dining. Near Union Square.
➕ K5 ✉ 545 Post Street ☎ 415/776–8135 🚌 2, 3, 4, 76

SLOW CLUB ($$)

Tough to find its home in Potrero Hill's warehouse district, but worth the effort. No reservations accepted.
➕ K8 ✉ 2501 Mariposa Street ☎ 415/241–9390 🚌 9, 22, 33

1751 SOCIAL CLUB ($$$)

Mission District restaurant, bar and nightclub, with fine-dining versions of favorites such as fried shrimp, blue cheese burgers and a succulent vegetable stew.
➕ G6 ✉ 1751 Fulton Street ☎ 415/441–1751 🕐 Dinner only 🚌 5, 43

BURGERS & CAFÉS

ART INSTITUTE CAFÉ ($)

Simple pasta dishes and assorted snacks can be consumed while enjoying the splendid view across to San Francisco Bay from Telegraph Hill.

✚ J3 ✉ 800 Chestnut Street
☎ 415/749–4567 ◷ Lunch only 🚌 15, 30, 41; Powell–Hyde cable car

DOTTIE'S TRUE BLUE CAFÉ ($)

Small, friendly diner close to Union Square with great start-the-day omelets and a variety of healthy lunches.

✚ K5 ✉ 522 Jones Street
☎ 415/885–2767
◷ Breakfast and lunch 🚌 27

LIVERPOOL LIL'S ($$)

It's a crime not to get a beer with your meal at this Pacific Heights saloon/burger joint. Dine on the sidewalk when weather permits.

✚ G4 ✉ 2942 Lyon Street
☎ 415/921–6664 🚌 30, 41, 45

MAX'S OPERA CAFÉ ($–$$)

While the New York style deli fare is affordable and filling, the real attraction is the opera-singing staff, who strut their stuff each evening.

✚ J6 ✉ 601 Van Ness Avenue
☎ 415/771–7301 🚌 5, 42, 47, 49

STEAK & SEAFOOD

AQUA ($$$$)

Carefully prepared and presented seafood draws a style-conscious crowd to this modernistic eatery on the edge of the Financial District.

✚ L4 ✉ 252 California Street
☎ 415/956–9662 🚌 1, 41; California Street cable car

BRAZEN HEAD ($$)

There's no sign outside this intimate Cow Hollow gem, decorated primarily with wood. Order the hearty peppercorn steak from the varied menu.

✚ H4 ✉ 3166 Buchanan Street
☎ 415/921–7600 ◷ Dinner only (until 1am) 🚌 22, 41, 45

FARALLON ($$$)

Fish dominates the decor and the menu of this downtown spot serving caviar, seared ahi, soft-shell crab and more. Aquatic features, like the octopus barstools, add to the "dinner as theater" concept.

✚ K5 ✉ 450 Post Street
☎ 415/956–6969 ◷ Dinner only Sun 🚌 2, 3, 4; Powell cable car

IZZY'S STEAK & CHOP HOUSE ($$–$$$)

A carnivore's paradise in the Marina focusing on steak in all cuts and sizes.

✚ H4 ✉ 3345 Steiner Street
☎ 415/563–0487 ◷ Dinner only 🚌 22, 76

PJ'S OYSTER BED ($$)

Located in the Sunset, PJ's features a Cajun-style menu with jazzy New Orleans winners like gumbo, barbecue oysters, jambalaya and blackened fish.

✚ E8 ✉ 737 Irving Street
☎ 415/566–7775 🚌 6, 43, 44, 66; also the N Judah

BEST BRUNCH BETS

Brunch is a Sunday social fixture for many San Franciscans, so prepare to go early or wait it out with the rest of the hungry hordes. Expect to pay $10–$20 per person, depending on the restaurant, of course, and the number of Bloody Marys you plan to imbibe. Mouth-watering spots in the city include Dottie's True Blue Café and Slow Club (see entries); Ella's (✉ 500 Presidio Avenue ☎ 415/441–5669), famous for its chicken hash; Kate's Kitchen (✉ 471 Haight Street ☎ 415/626–3984); and Mama's on Washington Square (✉ 1701 Stockton Street ☎ 415/362– 6421). Remember to bring the Sunday paper to distract you from your rumbling stomach.

Italian

COFFEE SAN FRANCISCO STYLE

San Franciscans place great importance on the quality of coffee. Cafés listed here are chosen for their food (➤ 84) for those suited to evening socializing), but most also pride themselves on the excellence of their coffee beans and serve the drink in several main forms. Besides espresso (coffee brewed at high pressure) and cappuccino (espresso topped by a creamy milk head), coffee is commonly served as *caffè latté* (espresso with steamed milk) and *caffè mocha* (espresso with chocolate).

ANTICA TRATTORIA ($$$)

One of the city's top trattorias located in Russian Hill; offers a regularly changing menu and good wine list.
➕ J4 ✉ 2400 Polk Street
☎ 415/928–5797 ⏰ Closed Mon 🚌 19, 41, 42, 45, 47, 76

CAPP'S CORNER ($$)

Owned by a former boxing champion, this North Beach spot has good inexpensive pasta lunches and offers five-course set dinners as well as a full menu.
➕ K4 ✉ 1600 Powell Street
☎ 415/989–2589 🚌 15, 30, 41, 45

DELFINA ($$)

A Mission District trattoria serving simple, delicious dishes with top-notch ingredients.
➕ J8 ✉ 3621 18th Street
☎ 415/552–4055 ⏰ Dinner only 🚇 16th Street Mission
🚌 14, 33

ENRICO'S ($$–$$$)

A prime people-watching location in North Beach with live music in the evening, plus a lengthy menu of Italian-American fare spanning risotto, ravioli pizzas and more.
➕ K4 ✉ 504 Broadway
☎ 415/982–6223 🚌 15, 30, 41

MARIO'S BOHEMIAN CIGAR STORE ($)

A long-established North Beach café that offers excellent *focaccia* bread snacks.
➕ K4 ✉ 566 Columbus Avenue ☎ 415/362–0536
🚌 15, 30, 41, 45

NORTH BEACH PIZZA ($)

The thick, chewy pizzas with a host of toppings, famous throughout the city, often result in a line outside in the evening; a newer branch is at 1310 Grant Avenue.
➕ K4 ✉ 1499 Grant Avenue
☎ 415/433–2444 🚌 15, 30, 41, 45

L'OSTERIA DEL FORNO ($)

North Beach establishment with excellent food and good wine served in authentic surroundings.
➕ K4 ✉ 519 Columbus Avenue ☎ 415/982–1124
⏰ Closed Tue 🚌 15, 30, 41

RISTORANTE MILANO ($$–$$$)

Freshly-prepared northern Italian fare and an intimate, rustic setting make this a memorable dinner spot.
➕ J4 ✉ 1448 Pacific Avenue
☎ 415/673–2961 ⏰ Dinner only 🚌 12

ROSE PISTOLA ($$$)

North Beach haunt with an open kitchen, wood-burning oven and menu inspired by the cuisine of Italy's Liguria region. Live jazz Sun–Thu.
➕ K4 ✉ 532 Columbus Avenue ☎ 415/399–0499
🚌 15, 30, 41

STEPS OF ROME

A festive North Beach atmosphere, complete with singing waiters, and a tempting range of pasta dishes and desserts.
➕ K4 ✉ 348 Columbus Avenue ☎ 415/397–0435
🚌 15, 30, 41

French

BAKER STREET BISTRO ($$)

Patrons tolerate cramped quarters in return for fantastic bistro fare at stunningly good prices.

➕ G4 ✉ 2953 Baker Street ☎ 415/931–1475 🕐 Closed Mon 🚌 41, 45, 76

CAFÉ BASTILLE ($)

A very effective re-creation of a stylish Parisian bistro in a Financial District alley.

➕ L5 ✉ 22 Belden Alley ☎ 415/986–5673 🚌 15

CAFÉ CLAUDE ($$)

Quintessentially French dishes like salad nicoise and onion soup are served in the downtown French quarter of the city, by Gallic waiters with a bit of attitude.

➕ L5 ✉ 7 Claude Lane (between Grant and Kearny streets) ☎ 415/392–3515 🚌 2, 3, 4, 15, 45

CAMPTON PLACE ($$$$)

An ever-changing menu reflects the fact that only the freshest local produce is used to create dishes especially valued for their natural flavors. Close to Union Square.

➕ K5 ✉ Campton Place Hotel, 340 Stockton Street ☎ 415/955–5555 🚌 30, 45

CLEMENTINE ($$)

A local anomaly, this bistro relishes in all things *français*, including inexpensive escargot.

➕ F6 ✉ 126 Clement Street ☎ 415/387–0408 🕐 Closed Mon 🚌 1, 2, 33, 38

FLEUR DE LYS ($$$$)

More formal than many—jacket and tie required—and serving San Francisco's best French food.

➕ K5 ✉ 777 Sutter Street ☎ 415/673–7779 🕐 Dinner only 🚌 2, 3, 4, 7

FRINGALE ($$$)

Basque-French cuisine dished up in an intimate but casual bistro setting close to the Metreon. Extensive and irresistible desserts.

➕ L6 ✉ 570 4th Street ☎ 415/543–0573 🕐 Closed Sun 🚇 Powell Street or Montgomery Street 🚌 9, 15, 30, 45

MASA'S ($$$$)

Californian-French restaurant on Nob Hill renowned for its quality. Usually reserved weeks in advance, although cancellations make tables available at short notice.

➕ K5 ✉ Vintage Court Hotel, 648 Bush Street ☎ 415/989–7154 🕐 Dinner only; closed Sun, Mon 🚌 2, 3, 4, 30, 76

PLOUF ($$)

A downtown bistro on a pedestrian-only alley where diners can eat outdoors. Tasty seafood is the focus; mussels are the house specialty.

➕ L5 ✉ 40 Belden Place ☎ 415/986–6491 🚌 1, 3, 4, 15, 30, 45, 76

TI COUZ ($)

Wash down sweet and savory crepes with tasty hard cider at this Mission District creperie.

➕ J8 ✉ 3108 16th Street ☎ 415/252–7373 🚇 16th Street Mission 🚌 14, 22, 26

SOURDOUGH BREAD

The slightly bitter and chewy sourdough bread served in many San Franciscan restaurants first appeared here during the Gold Rush (and was first baked commercially by a French San Franciscan settler called Isadore Boudin). Yeast and baking powder were scarce and settlers made bread using a sour starter, a fermented mixture of flour and water that enabled the dough to rise. San Franciscan folklore holds that the quality of a sourdough loaf is dependent upon environmental conditions–in particular, the local fog.

Asian

DIM SUM

Popular at lunchtime and weekend brunch, *dim sum* consists of various small dishes offered to diners from carts. The cost is determined by the number of empty dishes on your table. Favorite *dim sum* dishes include *cha sil bow*—steamed pork bun; *chern goon*—spring rolls; *gai bow*—steamed chicken bun; *sil mi*—steamed pork and shrimp dumpling. Less popular among Westerners are *gai guerk*—braised chicken feet; and *op guerk*—braised duck's feet. To sample some of these dishes try Chinatown eateries such as Hunan Home's (✉ 622 Jackson Street ☎ 415.982–2844); or Hing Lung (✉ 674 Broadway ☎ 415/398–8838) or, in the Richmond, Ton Kiang (➤ this page). For a slightly different selection of dishes, try the Financial District's pricey but excellent Yank Sing (✉ 101 Spear Street ☎ 415/957–9300).

CHINESE

BRANDY HO'S ($$)
Earning deserved acclaim for its Hunan cuisine; diners with delicate palates might find some of the spicier dishes at this Chinatown spot too hot to handle.
➕ K4–L4 ✉ 217 Columbus Avenue ☎ 415/788–7527
🚌 15, 30, 45, 83

ERIC'S RESTAURANT ($)
Delicious Hunan and Mandarin cuisine served in a clean white dining room overflowing with Noe Valley locals.
➕ J10 ✉ 1500 Church Street ☎ 415/282–0919 🚌 24; J

HOUSE OF NANKING ($)
Tiny, popular eatery in Chinatown—among the first to bring Shanghai and northern Chinese cooking to San Francisco.
➕ K4 ✉ 919 Kearny Street ☎ 415/421–1429 🚌 15

LUCKY CREATION ($)
Tiny Chinatown hideaway serving adventurous vegetarian, and a few vegan, versions of Chinese food, including *dim sum* at weekends.
➕ K4 ✉ 854 Washington Street ☎ 415/989–0818
🚌 45

TON KIANG ($$)
Spread over two Richmond District floors and frequented mainly for its excellent Hong Kong style *dim sum*, though also offering a predominantly Hakka-style dinner menu.
➕ D6 ✉ 5821 Geary Boulevard ☎ 415/387–8273
🚌 38

INDIAN

GAYLORD INDIA RESTAURANT ($$)
With great views across the Golden Gate from Russian Hill, specializing in northern Indian fare.
➕ J3 ✉ Ghirardelli Square, 900 North Point Street
☎ 415/771–8822 🚌 19, 42

INDIAN OVEN ($$)
Head chef Mohammed Aslam whips up some of the best tandoori, naan and curry dishes in town.
➕ H7 ✉ 233 Fillmore Street ☎ 415/626–1628 🕐 Dinner only 🚌 6, 7, 22, 66, 71

MAHARANI ($$)
Friendly Nob Hill Indian eatery with good prices and a menu including many vegetarian dishes.
➕ J5 ✉ 1122 Post Street ☎ 415/775–1988 🕐 Dinner only Tue 🚌 42

JAPANESE

ISOBUNE ($$)
Watch the chef prepare sushi, then make your selection from the many sushi-laden boats that float along the counter.
➕ H5 ✉ Japan Center, 1737 Post Street, Japantown ☎ 415/563–1030 🚌 2, 3, 4, 22, 38

KABUTO A&S ($$)
A no-frills atmosphere at this Richmond District sushi bar keeps the focus on fresh raw fish.
➕ D6 ✉ 5121 Geary Boulevard 🕐 Dinner only Sun; closed Mon ☎ 415/752–5652
🚌 2, 38

KYO-YA ($$$)

In keeping with the luxury of this Financial District hotel, Kyo-Ya serves some of the finest Japanese food in the city. Reserve ahead.
✚ L5 ✉ Sheraton Palace Hotel, 2 New Montgomery Street ☎ 415/546–5090 🕐 Closed Sun, Mon Ⓜ Montgomery Street 🚌 5, 6, 7, 8, 9, 21, 31, 38, 42, 45, 71

MIFUNE ($)

Fast food Japanese style, served to fast-moving customers; includes simple but excellent noodle dishes.
✚ H5 ✉ Japan Center, 737 Post Street, Japantown ☎ 415/922–0337 🚌 38

SINGAPOREAN

STRAITS CAFÉ ($$)

Offers a range of dishes that mix and match various Southeast Asian cuisines, including many vegetarian options and a strong choice of seafood dishes. Close to Golden Gate Park.
✚ F6 ✉ 3300 Geary Boulevard ☎ 415/668–1783 🚌 38

THAI

BASIL ($$–$$$)

Stark and modernistic decor and Thai food a cut above the less pricey offerings around the city with generally lighter, if no less spicy, dishes.
✚ K7 ✉ 1175 Folsom Street ☎ 415/552–8999 🚌 12, 19, 76

KHAN TOKE ($$)

A Richmond restaurant, where guests remove their shoes before dining on top-notch Thai cuisine at sunken tables.
✚ D6 ✉ 5937 Geary Boulevard ☎ 415/668–6654 🚌 2, 29, 38

THEP PHANOM ($)

Hot and authentic Thai cuisine. In the Lower Heights neighborhood.
✚ H7 ✉ 900 Waller Street ☎ 415/431–2526 🚌 6, 7, 66, 71, 73

VIETNAMESE

ANA MANDARA ($$–$$$)

Who would have thought that Vietnamese food in such elegant surroundings could exist in Ghirardelli Square? The upstairs bar is a perfect pre- or post-dinner spot.
✚ J3 ✉ 891 Beach Street ☎ 415/771–6800 🚌 19, 32, 42; Powell–Hyde cable car

LE COLONIAL ($$$)

The ambience evokes French-colonial Vietnam and a veranda beckons for fine-weather dining; sample a snack from the bar or sit down to fully experience the classy California re-workings of Vietnamese dishes.
✚ K5 ✉ 20 Cosmo Place ☎ 415/391–2233 🕐 Dinner only 🚌 1, 2, 3, 4, 27, 31, 76

FUSION

SILKS ($$$$)

A blend of contemporary American cuisine and Asian subtlety at this Financial District hotel.
✚ L5 ✉ Mandarin Oriental Hotel, 222 Sansome Street ☎ 415/986–2020 🚌 12, 42; California Street cable car

VEGETARIAN DELIGHTS

If you don't eat meat, you still have plenty of dining options in the City by the Bay. In addition to Greens (➤ 71), noteworthy vegetarian establishments include Ananda Fuara (✉ 1298 Market Street ☎ 415/621–1994), a vegan restaurant in the Civic Center, and Millennium (✉ 246 McAllister ☎ 415/ 487–9800), which serves imaginative organic and dairy-free entrees. Most Chinese and Indian restaurants also offer numerous vegetarian dishes.

Spanish, Mexican, Latin

BARGAIN BURRITOS

Taquerias dominate San Francisco's Mexican landscape, in large part because of the population's love affair with burritos, a folded flour tortilla stuffed with any or all of the following: rice, beans, lettuce, salsa, cheese, chicken, beef, sour cream and guacamole. You'll get the best burrito bang for your buck at these Mission District dives: Taqueria Cancun (see entry); La Cumbre Taqueria (✉ 515 Valencia Street ☎ 415/863–8205); La Taqueria (✉ 2889 Mission Street ☎ 415/285–7117); and Pancho Villa Taqueria (✉ 3071 16th Street ☎ 415/864–8840).

B44 ($$–$$$)

Paella and other Catalan cuisine on lovely Belden Lane, plus Spanish wines and outside tables.
✚ L5 ✉ 44 Belden Place ☎ 415/986–6287 ◑ Dinner only Sat; closed Sun ▤ 3, 4, 12, 15

CAFÉ MARIMBA ($$)

Crowded and colorful Marina restaurant. A delightful menu with an emphasis on fish.
✚ G4 ✉ 2317 Chestnut Street ☎ 415/776–1506 ◑ Dinner only Mon ▤ 28, 30, 76

CHARANGA ($–$$)

This bustling Mission eatery has a loyal following with its tasty Caribbean and Latin American-style tapas.
✚ J8 ✉ 2351 Mission Street ☎ 415/282–1813 ◑ Closed Sun, Mon ◉ 16th Street Mission ▤ 14, 26, 49

ESPERPENTO ($$)

Low prices and high energy in the Mission. Share a pitcher of sangria and listen to the mariachi band while you eat.
✚ J9 ✉ 3295 22nd Street ☎ 415/282–8867 ▤ 14, 26 ◉ 24th Street

HABANA ($$–$$$)

The "hand-crafted" Cuban cocktails add to the atmosphere of this Pacific Heights spot but the food is the real draw; contemporary versions of Cuban cuisine from guava-glazed ribs to plantain crusted tuna.
✚ J4 ✉ 2080 Van Ness Avenue ☎ 415/567–7606 ◑ Dinner only ▤ 12, 42, 47, 49, 76

LA RONDALLA ($–$$)

Mission hotspot known more for its margaritas and lively atmosphere than the food.
✚ J8 ✉ 901 Valencia Street ☎ 415/647–7474 ◑ Closed Mon ◉ 16th Street or 24th Street ▤ 14, 26

MAYA ($$$)

Both the food and the surroundings are elegant at this SoMa Mexican restaurant. Be prepared for French-food prices.
✚ L5 ✉ 303 2nd Street ☎ 415/543–2928 ◑ Dinner only Sat, Sun ◉ Montgomery Street ▤ 15, 30, 45

TAQUERIA CANCUN ($)

Burritos in many varieties and other low-cost, well-prepared Mexican favorites are found in this busy eatery in the Mission District.
✚ J8 ✉ 2288 Mission Street ☎ 415/252–9560 ▤ 14, 49

THIRSTY BEAR BREWING CO. ($$)

A large post-work crowd drink beer brewed on these SoMa premises. Hot and cold tapas, along with sandwiches and other Spanish entrees.
✚ L5 ✉ 661 Howard Street ☎ 415/974–0905 ◑ Dinner only Sun ◉ Montgomery Street ▤ 14, 15, 30, 45

ZARZUELA ($$–$$$)

If you can brave the dire parking situation in Russian Hill, the traditional Spanish tapas, paella and sangria are worth the effort.
✚ J4 ✉ 2000 Hyde Street ☎ 415/346–0800 ◑ Dinner only; closed Sun, Mon ▤ 41, 45; Powell–Hyde cable car

Potpourri

AXUM CAFÉ ($)
Flavorful, inexpensive Ethiopian concoctions in the Lower Haight; spicy entrees and an array of vegetarian options, along with numerous lamb and beef dishes.
✚ H7 ✉ 698 Haight Street ☎ 415/252-7912 🕐 Dinner only Tue 🚌 6, 7, 66, 71

CAFÉ PRAGUE ($–$$)
When the Italian flavor of North Beach becomes too familiar, drop into this small and decidedly casual spot serving soups, pastries and other options with east European, though rarely Czech, lineage; also boasts a house jazz band.
✚ K4 ✉ 584 Pacific Avenue ☎ 415/433-3811 🚌 12, 15, 41

GREENS ($$$)
Gourmet-pleasing dishes using the produce of an organic farm run at a Zen Buddhist retreat on the north side of San Francisco Bay. The bay views are as stunning as the food. Reserve ahead.
✚ H3 ✉ Building A, Fort Mason Center ☎ 415/771-6222 🚌 22, 28, 30, 47, 49

KAN ZAMAN ($–$$)
An inspired addition to the city's café scene just outside Golden Gate Park: the deep cushions, large hookahs and selection of Arabian snacks are memorable.
✚ F7 ✉ 1793 Haight Street ☎ 415/751-9656 🚌 6, 7, 33, 43, 66, 71

KATIA'S RUSSIAN TEA ROOM ($$)
Traditional dishes like beef stroganoff, blinis, caviar and borscht at one of the few Russian restaurants in San Francisco. A guitarist/accordionist livens up the atmosphere.
✚ E6 ✉ 600 5th Street ☎ 415/668-9292 🕐 Dinner only Sat, Sun; closed Mon 🚌 5, 21, 31, 44

KOKKARI ESTIATORIO ($$$)
Financial District taverna serving classic, expensive Greek favorites; *spanakopita* (spinach pie), moussaka and lamb dishes are just a few of the choices.
✚ L4 ✉ 200 Jackson Street ☎ 415/981-0983 🕐 Dinner only Sat; closed Sun 🚇 Embarcadero 🚌 12, 42

MATTERHORN SWISS RESTAURANT ($$–$$$)
Sweet and savory fondue is the main event, but patrons can also order sausage, schnitzel and other regional fare at this Russian Hill eatery.
✚ J4 ✉ 2323 Van Ness Avenue ☎ 415/885-6116 🕐 Dinner only; closed Mon 🚌 19, 41, 42, 45, 47, 49, 76

MITCHELL'S ICE CREAM ($)
Head to the Mission District on a warm, sunny day and this ice cream emporium is sure to be busy. You will find dozens of innovative flavors including pumpkin, purple yam and avocado.
✚ J10 ✉ 688 San Jose Avenue ☎ 415/648-2300 🚇 24th Street—Mission 🚌 26, 67

THE COMPLETE TEA

Afternoon tea costs around $20 and typically offers a choice of Earl Grey, orange pekoe, Darjeeling, jasmine, lapsang souchong, oolong, peppermint or chamomile tea, to be served with any or all of the following: sandwiches (filled with bacon, cucumber, smoked salmon, ham, or egg and parsley), scones and fancy pastries. The first item to be eaten should be the palate-cleansing cucumber sandwiches. Consider making reservations at the luxurious Compass Rose (✉ Westin St. Francis, 335 Powell Street ☎ 415/774-0167); the Garden Court (✉ Sheraton Place Hotel, 2 New Montgomery Street ☎ 415/512-1111), which has the city's most ornate interior; Imperial Teacourt (✉ 1411 Powell Street ☎ 415/788-6080), one of the country's few traditional Chinese teahouses; the Ritz-Carlton (✉ 600 Stockton Street ☎ 415/296-7465), where tea is accompanied by a harpist; or the Neiman Marcus Rotunda (✉ 150 Stockton Street ☎ 415/362-4777), which includes a bird's-eye view of Union Square.

Department Stores & Shopping Centers

CROCKER GALLERIA

Designer clothing stores, food shops and snack stands make this small, chic shopping mall in the Financial District ideal for idle browsing.

➕ L5 ✉ 50 Post Street
☎ 415/393–1505
🚌 2, 3, 4, 5, 6

EMBARCADERO CENTER

A three-level shopping complex spanning eight city blocks; pick up a free map to plot a course around the walkways, plazas and scores of interesting stores.

➕ L4 ✉ Battery Street, between Clay and Sacramento streets ☎ 415/772–0700
🚌 1, 41, 42

GHIRARDELLI SQUARE

A chocolate factory thoughtfully converted to house a range of entertaining stores, all with merchandise a cut above the standard tourist items found elsewhere in the neighborhood.

➕ J3 ✉ 900 North Point Street ☎ 415/775–5500
🚌 19, 30, 42

JAPAN CENTER

From kimonos to rice cookers, Japanese arts and crafts are well represented in this complex of stores, restaurants and offices.

➕ H5 ✉ Post Street, between Laguna and Fillmore streets 🚌 2, 3, 4, 38

MACY'S WEST

Occupying two sites on either side of O'Farrell Street, Macy's carries a large stock of quality clothing and much more, not least an inviting array of edibles in the basement food emporium.

➕ K5 ✉ 170 O'Farrell Street
☎ 415/397–3333 🚌 2, 3, 4, 30, 38, 45

NEIMAN MARCUS

Fine china, dazzling jewelry and racks of formal evening wear confirm Neiman Marcus as the preferred shopping stop for the wealthy.

➕ K5 ✉ 150 Stockton Street
☎ 415/362–3900 🚌 2, 3, 4, 30, 38, 45

NORDSTROM

A pianist tickles the ivories as shoppers move across this huge store's five floors, whose stock includes a massive selection of shoes.

➕ K5 ✉ San Francisco Shopping Center, 865 Market Street ☎ 415/243–8500
🚇 Powell Street 🚌 5, 6, 7, 8, 9, 21, 31, 66, 71

SAKS FIFTH AVENUE

Less ostentatious than its rivals, Saks offers a strong selection of clothes at prices that may not be low but are reasonable for the quality.

➕ K5 ✉ 220 Post Street
☎ 415/986–4300 🚌 2, 3, 4, 30; Powell–Hyde or Powell–Mason cable car

SAN FRANCISCO SHOPPING CENTRE

An architecturally innovative home for 80 diverse stores.

➕ K5 ✉ 865 Market Street
☎ 888/697–7733 🚇 Powell Street 🚌 5, 6, 7, 8, 9, 21, 31, 66, 71

Discount Outlets & Bargain Stores

ALEMANY FLEA MARKET
Wacky furniture, bizarre apparel and all manner of curiosities are liable to be found at this once weekly gathering.
➕ Off map to south ✉ 100 Alemany Boulevard ☎ 415/674–2043 🕐 Sun only 🚌 9X, 23, 24, 67

BASIC BROWN BEARS
Open daily, this factory, which makes teddy bears and other small and soft items for children, offers its products at discounted rates and takes customers on a tour of the manufacturing process.
➕ J3 ✉ The Cannery, 2801 Leavenworth Street ☎ 866/588–BEAR 🚌 32

BURLINGTON COAT FACTORY
This outlet carries the obvious coats, but in addition to clothing, it boasts a sizable selection of cut-price shoes.
➕ L6 ✉ 899 Howard Street ☎ 415/495–7234 🚌 12

CRIS
A welcome surprise for budget-conscious shoppers in the usually expensive Pacific Heights neighborhood, with an array of designer names; most for women though with small menswear section.
➕ J3 ✉ 2056 Polk Street ☎ 415/474–1191 🚌 19

CROSSROADS TRADING STORE
Wide range of used clothing, accessories and jewelry for men and women, with a youthful bias. There are several locations in and around San Francisco.
➕ H5 ✉ 1901 Fillmore Street ☎ 415/775–8885 🚌 2, 3, 4, 22, 76

GOOD BYES
Great range of designer business clothing and a lesser amount of casual-wear, for women and men.
➕ F6 ✉ 3464 Sacramento Street ☎ 415/346–6388 🚌 1, 4, 43

GOODWILL INDUSTRIES
Just one of many branches of this proceeds-to-charity chain, well-stocked with donated clothes, books and assorted other items from coffee tables to novelty wall hangings.
➕ H5 ✉ 1700 Fillmore Street ☎ 415/441–2159 🚌 38

RED DOT
Wide ranging assortment of stylish and modern designer womenswear, including sportswear, at much less than retail prices. Smaller branch at 2176 Chestnut Street.
➕ L6 ✉ 508 4th Street ☎ 415/979–1597 🚌 15

THRIFT TOWN
Packed from floor to ceiling with donated secondhand clothing, furniture, books and lots more, this is one of the largest of San Francisco's thrift stores. Many others are listed in the phone book.
➕ J8 ✉ 2101 Mission Street ☎ 415/861–1132 🚇 16th Street Mission 🚌 14, 49

SOMA REVIVED
SoMa highlights the ever-changing nature of San Francisco. In the late 1800s, while the city's rich were building palatial homes on Nob Hill, the flatlands south of Market Street (the area known as SoMa, ➤ 53) were exclusively the domain of the laboring classes; loading rail and sea cargo continued as SoMa's staple occupation until the 1970s. As the old industries declined, artists moved into the area's abandoned warehouses, later to be followed by many of the city's discount outlet stores and in the 1990s by media and internet companies. The leading design companies that occupy the numerous factory-outlet stores, sell their damaged or discontinued lines at 20 to 50 percent less than the cost in regular stores.

Antiques, Art & Collectibles

ANTIQUE JACKSON SQUARE

An historic area with rich pickings for antiques searchers, Jackson Square is a compact grouping of mostly brick-built 19th-century structures. The upper levels hold offices, while much of the street level is occupied by the stores. Bargains may be few, but 18th- and 19th-century European dressing tables, armchairs and chests of drawers, fine Asian tapestries and decorative pieces are in plentiful supply.

ANDREA SCHWARTZ GALLERY

There is always something new to see across this large exhibition space devoted to conteporary painting, installations and mixed media.

✚ L6 ✉ 525 2nd Street
☎ 415/495–2090 ▯ 10, 15

THE ENCHANTED CRYSTAL

Crystal and glass artfully crafted into decorative objects and jewelry.

✚ H4 ✉ 1895 Union Street
☎ 415/885–1335 ▯ 41, 45

FOLK ART INTERNATIONAL & BORETTI AMBER

Decorative items created from amber gathered in northern California sit alongside handicrafts and jewelry from Africa and Asia.

✚ J3 ✉ 140 Maiden Lane
☎ 415/392–9999 ▯ 19, 42

FUMIKI

Japanese *netsuke* and *obi* (the sash for a kimono), Chinese porcelain and Korean furniture are among the exquisite Far Eastern artifacts to be found in this copiously filled shop.

✚ L5 ✉ 272 Sutter Street
☎ 415/362–6677 ▯ 41, 45

GUMP'S

Held in high esteem by discerning San Franciscans since 1861 with antiques coming from all over the world, particularly Asia. An art gallery specializes in the works of emergent artists and another room is devoted to jade.

✚ L5 ✉ 135 Post Street
☎ 415/982–1616
▯ 2, 3, 4, 76

HANG ART

Displays what it believes is the cream of the new crop of Bay Area artists in two neighboring spacious galleries.

✚ K5 ✉ 556 and 567 Sutter Street ☎ 415/434–4264
▯ 1, 3, 38

JOHN BERGGRUEN GALLERY

Some of the leading names of 20th-century American art are likely to be found through the three floors of this highly-regarded gallery, which also features selected Europeans. Budget big if you are thinking of buying.

✚ K5 ✉ 228 Grant Avenue
☎ 415/781–4629 ▯ 2, 3, 4, 76

LANG ANTIQUES

Diverse, high-quality merchandize ranging from silverware and watches to Russian artworks.

✚ K5 ✉ 323 Sutter Street
☎ 415/982–2213
▯ 2, 3, 4, 76

LOLA GALLERY

Rejects the traditional white-walled gallery space in favor of five themed salons presenting new work from new artists whose diverse and eclectic pieces might span paintings, sculpture, music, film and literature.

✚ J9 ✉ 2517 Mission Street
☎ 415/401–6800 ▯ 14, 49

Bookstores

A CLEAN WELL-LIGHTED PLACE FOR BOOKS

The city's leading outlet for the newest fiction, be it mainstream or avant-garde, and a selection of nonfiction (► 85).

➕ J6 ✉ 601 Van Ness Avenue ☎ 415/441–6670 🚌 42, 47, 49

A DIFFERENT LIGHT

Generously stocked with fiction and nonfiction titles primarily of interest to gay men, with a section of lesbian-related writing.

➕ H8 ✉ 489 Castro Street ☎ 415/431–0891 🚌 24

THE BOOKSMITH

Contains an excellent range of recent general titles on most subjects, plus several shelves devoted to Californian travel and San Franciscan history.

➕ G7 ✉ 1644 Haight Street ☎ 415/863–8688 🚌 6, 7, 33, 43, 66, 71

BORDERS BOOKS AND MUSIC

Local branch of this fast growing nationwide chain, which stocks a massive selection of general fiction and nonfiction titles with an atmosphere conducive to browsing.

➕ K5 ✉ 400 Post Street ☎ 415/399–1633 🚌 2, 3, 4, 76

CITY LIGHTS

A publishing company and bookstore, inextricably linked to the 1950s' Beat Generation, founded by poet Lawrence Ferlinghetti. The stock includes many of the movement's definitive writings, fiction and nonfiction, and literary magazines.

➕ K4 ✉ 261 Columbus Avenue ☎ 415/362–8193 🚌 15, 41, 83

NATIONAL PARK STORE

Books, magazines and videos devoted to wild California and the natural history of the American West.

➕ K2–K3 ✉ Pier 39, Fisherman's Wharf ☎ 415/433–7221 🚌 32

PSYCHIC EYE BOOKS

A New Age store specializing in topics such as self-help, health and healing, philosophy and the occult.

➕ J6 ✉ 301 Fell Street ☎ 415/863–9997 🚌 21

STACEY'S BOOKSTORE

Four floors house an extensive selection of magazines and books on all subjects. Pluses include frequent author readings, gift wrapping and a helpful staff.

➕ L5 ✉ 581 Market Street ☎ 415/421–4687 🚇 Montgomery Street 🚌 2, 5, 6, 7, 9, 21, 31, 66, 71

WILLIAM K. STOUT ARCHITECTURAL BOOKS

Architectural tomes in sufficient quantity to attract both the professional architect and the interested amateur.

➕ L4 ✉ 804 Montgomery Street ☎ 415/391–6757 🚌 15, 41

SECONDHAND BOOKS

Besides offering plentiful outlets for new titles, San Francisco has numerous used-bookstores in which dedicated bibliophiles can spend many hours of happy browsing. Recommended stops include Forever After (✉ 1475 Haight Street ☎ 415/431–8299), with diverse fiction and nonfiction; the Argonaut Book Shop (✉ 788 Sutter Street ☎ 415/474–9067), especially strong on San Francisco history, with prices to match the rarity value of many items; and Book Bay (✉ Building C, Fort Mason Center ☎ 415/771–1076), where former library stock is sold at discount prices. Green Apple Books and Music (✉ 506 Clement Street ☎ 415/387–2272) carries a varied new and used collection of both.

Clothes

CLOTHES OF UNUSUAL SIZE

Anyone whose dimensions differ from the average can search for new clothes in San Francisco with confidence. Apparel for large men is the business of Rochester Big And Tall (✉ 700 Mission Street ☎ 415/982–6455) and Harper Greer (✉ 580 4th Street ☎ 415/543–4066) stocks elegant items in the larger ladies' sizes.

ANNIE'S

Just off Fillmore Street, this hip Pacific Heights boutique carries clothing by Chaiken, How & Wen and Katayone Adeli, among other known labels.
✚ H5 ✉ 2512 Sacramento Street ☎ 415/292–7164
🚌 1, 22

BANANA REPUBLIC

Noted for its predominantly lightweight, natural-fiber clothing in a range of earth tones for men and women, this enormous flagship store offers stylish, comfortable attire for contemporary urban living.
✚ K5 ✉ 256 Grant Avenue
☎ 415/788–3087
🚌 2, 3, 4

CHANEL BOUTIQUE

Two floors filled with clothes, cosmetics and much more from the renowned French designer are available for the woman with refined taste.
✚ L5 ✉ 155 Maiden Lane
☎ 415/981–1550
🚌 2, 3, 4, 30, 45

EMPORIO ARMANI

Top-quality business and casual clothing for stylish men and women, offered in a boutique setting complete with cappuccino bar.
✚ L5 ✉ 1 Grant Avenue
☎ 415/677–9400 🚌 5, 6, 7, 8, 9, 21, 31, 38

THE HOUND

Offers expensive, high-quality menswear, much of it based on popular perceptions of what an English country gentleman likes to wear; perfectionists can have their shirts made to measure.
✚ L5 ✉ 140 Sutter Street
☎ 415/989–0429
🚌 2, 3, 4, 76

OOMA

Bright and breezy designer womenswear and accessories ranging from polka-dot bikinis to flower-clad shoes, all of the items reflecting the vibrant taste of ooma's ('objects of my affection') owner.
✚ K4 ✉ 1422 Grant Avenue
☎ 415/627–6963
🚌 15, 41

ROLO SOMA

Many Rolo designs take their inspiration from street fashion, conjuring up expensive and extrovert attire for the daring man or woman who wishes to appear hip on the social circuit.
✚ K7 ✉ 1235 Howard Street
☎ 415/355–1122
🚌 12

WILKES BASHFORD

You will find classy men and women's clothing across the six impressively well-stocked floors of Wilkes Bashford. The suit section offers complimentary wine or imported mineral water to refresh customers who may be dithering over the crucial decision of what to buy.
✚ K5 ✉ 375 Sutter Street
☎ 415/986–4380
🚌 2, 3, 4, 30, 45, 76

Accessories & Used Clothes

ACCESSORIES

DHARMA
Inventive, one-of-a-kind, jewelry and other items fuse the counterculture influences of Haight-Ashbury with the arts and crafts of the Third World.
➕ G7 ✉ 1600 Haight Street
☎ 415/621–5597 🚌 6, 7, 33, 43, 66, 71

HERMÈS OF PARIS
Nothing comes cheap at this exceedingly fancy international chain featuring fashions from the famous French designer, but the belts, scarves, gloves and handbags are small images of perfection.
➕ K5 ✉ 212 Stockton Street
☎ 415/391–7200
🚌 2, 3, 4, 30, 45

TIFFANY & CO
A branch of the revered New York jewelry giant with more glittering stones than many people can dream about, and a dazzling display of gold and silver ornaments.
➕ K5 ✉ 350 Post Street
☎ 415/781–7000
🚌 2, 3, 4, 76

USED CLOTHES

AARDVARK'S
If you're looking for a choice of styles from many eras, you will be rewarded by a visit here to the pick of Haight-Ashbury's innumerable used clothing outlets.
➕ G7 ✉ 1501 Haight Street
☎ 415/621–3141 🚌 6, 7, 33, 43, 66, 71

BUFFALO EXCHANGE
If you tire of the clothes you are wearing, this is the place to trade them in and walk out dressed in something different; there is always clothing that is just in, or just out, to be picked up for a song—or for a trade-in deal.
➕ G7 ✉ 1555 Haight Street
☎ 415/431–7733 🚌 6, 7, 33, 43, 66, 71

LA ROSA
Should a formal dinner invitation unexpectedly fall into your hands, this is the place to hire or buy evening wear that has already seen its share of social occasions; the oldest items generally date from the 1920s.
➕ F7 ✉ 1711 Haight Street
☎ 415/668–3744 🚌 6, 7, 33, 43, 66, 71

VER UNICA
A mighty stock of mens and womens vintage wear plus shoes, handbags and assorted accessories.
➕ J6 ✉ 437B Hayes Street
☎ 415/431–0688 🚌 21

WORN OUT WEST
What started out fulfilling the sartorial needs of gay men in pursuit of the cowboy look has evolved into a cornucopia of high-quality used western wear, from Stetson hats and snakeskin boots to exceptionally attractive bolo ties.
➕ H8 ✉ 582 Castro Street
☎ 415/431–6020
🚌 24

MARKETS
Though San Francisco is not known for its markets, fresh fruit, vegetables and a small amount of seafood can be found at the Farmers' Market held at Larkin Street (between Grove and McAllister streets) every Wednesday and Sunday from 7am. Largest is the Farmers' Market at the Ferry Plaza, facing the Ferry Building, on Saturday from 8am and on Tuesday, Thursday and Sunday from 10am, featuring unusual, organic produce. Avid marketgoers might also like to test their mettle amid the densely packed throng on the Chinatown section of Stockton Street every weekday and Saturday when, it seems, the city's entire Chinese-American population arrives to stock up.

Offbeat

CHINATOWN STORES

Exotic, entertaining and often great value, the stores of Chinatown are among the most interesting in the city. Locals crowd the market stalls along Stockton Street, but nearby Grant Avenue holds visitor-aimed emporia stuffed with anything and everything Asian, from $500 jade ornaments to richly decorated 25-cent chopsticks. More practical but equally intriguing retailers include numerous herbalists and the Wok Shop (✉ 718 Grant Avenue), which sells a good line of fearsome meat cleavers.

AQUA SURF SHOP

Only hardcore surfers brave the cool San Francisco waters, but if you want to join them get the necessary here.
✚ Off map ✉ 2830 Stoat Boulevard ☎ 415/242–9283 🚇 18, 23, L

CLARION MUSIC CENTER

Regulars might rent a violin or cello, but casual visitors can content themselves with a stroll along the racks browsing the wonderful Asian musical instruments, which range from Burmese temple bells to Chinese egg rattles.
✚ K4 ✉ 816 Sacramento Street ☎ 415/391–1317 🚇 15, 30, 45

CANTON BAZAAR

One of several packed-to-the-gills stores in Chinatown offering everything from neighborhood posters and decorated chopsticks to cooking utensils and oversize statuary.
✚ K4 ✉ 1616 Grant Avenue ☎ 415/363–5750 🚇 30, 41, 45

DE VERA

Vases, necklaces and glassworks, from expensive 19th-century items to the almost affordable work of local artists; all of it a fine addition to any mantelpiece.
✚ K5 ✉ 28 Maiden Lane ☎ 415/788–0828 🚇 10

GLOBAL EXCHANGE

Store of a human rights organization offering clothing, artworks, and much more from the Third World guaranteed not to be produced in sweatshops or in environmentally destructive ways.
✚ J8 ✉ 2017 Mission Street ☎ 415/255–7296 🚇 16th Street–Mission 🚇 14, 49

MOONES

Modern furnishings, lighting and artworks with the accent fully on modern, created by cutting-edge designers.
✚ K8 ✉ 2412 Harrison Street ☎ 415/845–9746 🚇 12

NEEDLES & PENS

Clothes and other one-off creations from local and would-be artists, plus a gigantic stock of offbeat independent magazines and local rant and rave magazines published on a shoestring.
✚ J7 ✉ 483 14th Street ☎ 415/255–1534 🚇 16th Street–Mission 🚇 26

PIPE DREAMS

This survivor of Haight-Ashbury's 1960s hippie days continues to cater to the needs of the adventurous smoker and anyone in search of psychedelic ephemera.
✚ G7 ✉ 1376 Haight Street ☎ 415/431–3553 🚇 6, 7, 33, 43, 66, 71

RUSSKA BABUSHKA DOLLS

Sells a colossal collection of odd items from the former Soviet Union, from hammer-and-sickle T-shirts to elaborate tapestries.
✚ K2–K3 ✉ Pier 39, Fisherman's Wharf ☎ 415/788–7043 🚇 32

Miscellaneous

ADOLPH GASSER

Spread across 16,000sq ft (1,488sq m) of retail space, you will find here the largest stock of photographic equipment in northern California.

➕ L5 ✉ 181 2nd Street
☎ 415/495–3852
🚌 12, 15

CARDS AND COMICS CENTRAL

Not only a massive selection of comics but also related phenomena such as models, action figures and comic-related card games.

➕ D6 ✉ 5424 Geary Boulevard ☎ 415/668–3544
🚌 18, 38

COMP USA

San Franciscans looking for the latest software or just computer equipment, generally swear by the quality and low prices found here. Even if you don't intend to buy, its good for a browse to see what the wizards of Silicon Valley are up to.

➕ K5 ✉ 750 Market Street
☎ 415/391–9778 🚌 6, 7, 8, 9, 21, 31, 38, 66, 71

CRYSTAL WAY

Crystals in all shapes, colors and sizes, displayed and sold here for their healing qualities; customers can also partake of astrology and tarot readings.

➕ H8 ✉ 2335 Market Street
☎ 415/861–6511 🚋 Castro Street 🚌 37

FOTO-GRAPHIX BOOKS

Operated by the Friends of Photography Organisation and holding an extensive collection of lavishly illustrated photography-related books and other items with photographic themes.

➕ K6 ✉ 655 Mission Street
☎ 415/495–7242 🚋 Powell Street 🚌 14, 45, 71

FTC

Expansive stock of cutting-edge skateboards and skateboard spares, plus skate accessories that include hats, T-shirts and shoes.

➕ G7 ✉ 1632 Haight Street
☎ 415/626–0663 🚌 6, 7, 33, 43, 66, 71

MUSEUMSTORE

An exemplary collection of art-related books, posters and souvenirs.

➕ L5 ✉ San Francisco Museum of Modern Art, 151 3rd Street ☎ 415/357–4135
🚌 12, 15, 30, 45, 76

SEPHORA

A visual explosion of color accompanies the high-end cosmetics and fragrances here, from companies such as Hard Candy, Stila and Christian Dior.

➕ K5 ✉ 33 Powell Street
☎ 415/362–9360 🚋 Powell Street 🚌 30, 45

TEN REN TEA COMPANY

To the delight of visiting tea *aficionados*, this Chinatown store is packed with over 40 different blends from around the world. Taste before you buy.

➕ K4 ✉ 949 Grant Avenue
☎ 415/362–0656
🚌 15, 30, 41

COFFEE TO GO

The city's preponderance of cafés has helped make San Franciscans knowledgable and discerning coffee drinkers. The expertize extends to the purchase of coffee for brewing at home, and the city has acquired several highly regarded outlets for what has been termed "gourmet coffee." One of the most popular is Peet's Coffee and Tea (✉ 2156 Chestnut Street), who have been roasting and brewing coffee in the Bay Area since 1966, and stock beans from around the coffee-growing world together with a formidable variety of grinders and espresso machines. Other locations include:

✉ 22 Battery Street; ✉ 2197 Fillmore Street; ✉ 2257 Market Street; ✉ 2139 Polk Street; ✉ 217 Montgomery Street. It is always worth checking their website at www.peets.com).

Classical Music & Performing Arts

TICKETS

The major ticket agency, Ticketmaster, has numerous outlets at various locations including the following: the TIX booth on Union Square (see below); local branches of Tower Records and Wherehouse Music. For a credit card booking or recorded information ☎ 415/421–TIXS. TIX offers half-price day of performance tickets (cash only) for Bay Area arts events from a marked booth on the southwest side of Union Square (☎ 415/433–7827).

CLUB FUGAZI

A zany revue, *Beach Blanket Babylon*, has been running for more than 30 years at this North Beach venue, and continues to sell out.
✚ K4 ✉ 678 Green Street
☎ 415/421–4222
🚍 15, 30, 41, 45

CURRAN THEATRE

One of several mainstream theaters on Geary Street; top choice for Broadway blockbusters.
✚ K5 ✉ 445 Geary Street
☎ 415/551–2075 🚍 38

GEARY THEATER

The main base of the American Conservatory Theater; the highly professional and thought-provoking productions are well regarded among theatergoers and critics alike.
✚ K5 ✉ 415 Geary Street
☎ 415/749–2228 🚍 38

HERBST THEATRE

Chamber music, recitals and lectures throughout the year, and the springtime New and Unusual series from the San Francisco Symphony.
✚ J6 ✉ War Veterans' Building, 401 Van Ness Avenue
☎ 415/392–4400 🚍 Civic Center or Van Ness 🚍 5, 10, 20, 21, 42, 47, 49, 60, 70, 80

LOUISE M. DAVIES SYMPHONY HALL

Home of the San Francisco Symphony orchestra, whose season runs September to June. Summer appearances include a composer's festival, a pops series and other special performances.
✚ J6 ✉ 201 Van Ness Avenue
☎ 415/864–6000 🚍 Van Ness or Civic Center 🚍 5, 10, 20, 21, 42, 47, 49, 60, 70, 80

MAGIC THEATER

This small theater has an excellent reputation and stages productions ranging from children's plays to political satire.
✚ H3 ✉ Building D, Fort Mason Center ☎ 415/441–8822; information 415/441–8001 🚍 22, 28, 30, 47, 49

THEATER RHINOCEROS

The home of the US's first gay and lesbian theater company; the diverse offerings often explore social attitudes and behavior.
✚ J8 ✉ 2926 16th Street
☎ 415/861–5079 🚍 16th Street Mission 🚍 14, 22, 26, 33, 49

WAR MEMORIAL OPERA HOUSE

The venue for the San Francisco Opera season (Sep–Dec). Tickets are sold in advance; a limited number are available two hours before a performance. February to May, the San Francisco Ballet appears here and returns at Christmas for the *Nutcracker*.
✚ J6 ✉ 301 Van Ness Avenue
☎ 415/621–6600 🚍 Van Ness or Civic Center 🚍 5, 10, 20, 21, 42, 47, 49, 60, 70, 80

YERBA BEUNA CENTER FOR THE ARTS

State-of-the art venue with a strong program of contemporary music, dance and drama.
✚ L5 ✉ 710 Mission Street
☎ 415/392–2787 🚍 Powell Street 🚍 15, 30, 45, 78

Rock, Jazz & Blues

BOOM BOOM ROOM
No-frills funk, jazz and blues are performed by local and national artists at this Fillmore Street venue. Founded by legendary blues guitarist John Lee Hooker.

H5 ✉ 1601 Fillmore Street
☎ 415/673–8000
🚌 22, 38

THE FILLMORE
The legendary venue of the psychedelic era, revamped and showcasing Bay Area and internationally known rock bands.

H5 ✉ 1805 Geary Boulevard ☎ 415/346–6000
🚌 38

GREAT AMERICAN MUSIC HALL
Eclectic performers and a lavish setting replete with two bars, a balcony and marble columns.

J5 ✉ 859 O'Farrell Street
☎ 415/885–0750
🚌 19, 38

HOTEL UTAH SALOON
In business since 1908, the saloon's recent years have been spent as a venue for diverse live music from performers who do not mind a small stage within touching distance of most of the audience.

L6 ✉ 500 4th Street
☎ 415/546–6300 🚌 30, 76

THE INDEPENDENT
Comfortable mid-sized venue for mainstream rock, jazz and hip-hop talent from the Bay Area and very far beyond.

H7 ✉ 628 Divisadero Street ☎ 415/771–1421
🚌 24

JAZZ AT PEARL'S
This enjoyable jazz spot draws an informed and appreciative crowd, and is a likely place to catch the hottest local, and often national, names.

K4 ✉ 256 Columbus Avenue ☎ 415/291–8255
🚌 41, 83

LOU'S PIER 47
The top-notch blues performers who regularly appear here draw appreciative audiences. Two shows daily.

J3 ✉ 300 Jefferson Street
☎ 415/771–5687 🚌 32; Powell–Hyde cable car

RASSELAS
At this combined jazz and supper club you can savor Ethiopian food and listen to some of the better local combos.

G5 ✉ 1534 Fillmore Street
☎ 415/346–8696 🚌 1, 4

THE SALOON
This spit-and-sawdust saloon, with a history that reaches back to the 1800s, makes a great backdrop for no-frills performances by rock and blues bands.

K4 ✉ 1232 Grant Avenue
☎ 415/989–7666 🚌 15, 41, 45, 83

SLIM'S
The excellent sound system and convivial atmosphere make this one of the city's best club-size music spots for quality rock, jazz or rhythm and blues acts every night.

K7 ✉ 333 11th Street
☎ 415/255–0333 🚌 9, 42

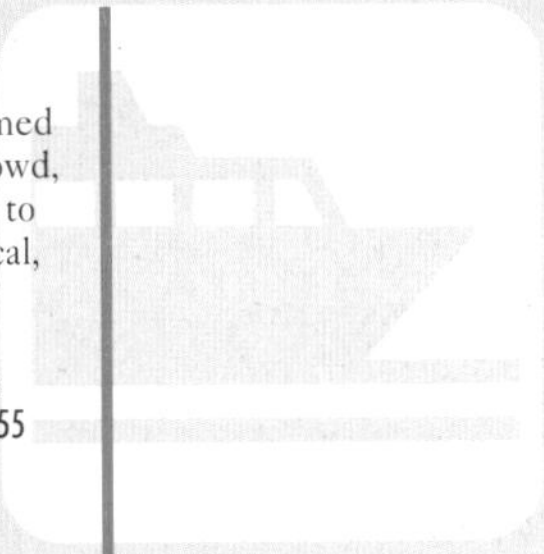

BLUES BY THE BAY

Over a weekend each September, the San Francisco Blues Festival brings some of the genre's leading exponents to daylong open-air concerts at Great Meadow, near Fort Mason Center. The enjoyable and relaxed event has been taking place for over 30 years. For ticket details
☎ 415/979–5588; website www.sfblues.com

Nightclubs

GUIDED NIGHTCLUBBING

If deciding where to strut your stuff in the San Franciscan night proves impossible, you might relish the assistance of Three Babes and a Bus (☎ 800/414–0158), a company that will carry you—and a busload of similarly indecisive individuals—on a four-hour tour of some of the city's hottest nightspots (Saturdays only). The $35 price includes admission and special ID allowing you to walk straight in, even when there is a line of people waiting to get in.

BIMBO'S 365 CLUB

Drawing crowds for nearly 70 years, this spacious North Beach club entertains with swingers, crooners and the occasional rocker.
✚ K3 ✉ 1025 Columbus Avenue ☎ 415/474–0365 🚌 15, 30, 41, 45

CAFÉ DU NORD

Hipster San Franciscans quaff cocktails in this basement bar as they enjoy swing, jazz and salsa performers.
✚ H7 ✉ 2170 Market Street ☎ 415/861–5016 🚌 37; F

ELBO ROOM

Shoot pool downstairs, or pay a small cover for live music upstairs; acts range from Latin salsa to hip-hop.
✚ J8 ✉ 647 Valencia Street ☎ 415/552–7788 🚌 16th Street Mission 🚌 14, 26, 49

THE END UP

The biggest and most dependable of a number of gay- and lesbian-oriented nightspots, with riotous dance music.
✚ L6 ✉ 401 6th Street ☎ 415/646–0999 🚌 27, 42

FLUID ULTRA LOUNGE

Starkly minimalist setting offset by computer-controlled floor-lighting that creates changing colors and shapes, this club attracts top DJs and a clientele of the cool and the curious.
✚ L5 ✉ 662 Mission Street ☎ 415/615–6888 🚌 14, 45, 71

NICKIE'S BBQ

Groove to DJ music with other energetic dancers in this tiny, packed spot in the dodgy Lower Haight. Lots of soul, funk, hi-hop and jungle.
✚ H7 ✉ 460 Haight Street ☎ 415/621–6508 🚌 6, 7, 22, 66, 71

1015 FOLSOM

DJ John Digweed and other big names in the business spin techno at this multi-floor, after-hours SoMa club.
✚ K6 ✉ 1015 Folsom Street (at 6th Street) ☎ 415/431–1200 🚌 12, 27, 42

RUBY SKYE

Sip a cocktail in the jungle room or the VIP room, or hit the packed dance floor. Both DJs and live bands perform here, depending on the night.
✚ K5 ✉ 420 Mason Street ☎ 415/693–0777 🚌 2, 3, 4, 38, 76

SNO-DRIFT

When the diners move away, this pseudo-alpine lodge becomes a fashionable and pricey nightspot with diverse musical themes and some of the city's best DJs.
✚ M8 ✉ 1830 3rd Street ☎ 415/431–4766 🚌 15

VELVET LOUNGE

Pulsating sounds of the 70s, 80, 90s plus 21st-century dance mixed with lashings of salsa, soul and other rhythmic offerings served to an unpretentious crowd.
✚ L4 ✉ 443 Broadway ☎ 415/788–0288 🚌 12

Bars

CARNELIAN ROOM

A stylish and smart (evening only) bar on this landmark building's 52nd floor, with wonderful sunset views across the city.
✚ L5 ✉ Bank of America Center, 555 California Street ☎ 415/433–7500 🚃 15, 42; California Street cable car

DRAGON BAR

Lush tones of deep red and black, and faux-Asian motifs decorate this trendy North Beach bar-cum-nightclub where the city's grooviest souls come to be seen.
✚ K4 ✉ 473 Broadway ☎ 415/834–9383 🚃 12, 15, 30, 41

LI PO

A cavelike entrance leads into this Chinatown bar, where the over-the-top decor seems less extreme after a few Chinese Tsing Tao beers.
✚ K4 ✉ 916 Grant Avenue ☎ 415/982–0072 🚃 1, 15, 30, 45

PIED PIPER

Sip a cocktail in subdued surroundings and gaze at the immense Maxfield Parrish picture behind the bar.
✚ L5 ✉ Sheraton Palace Hotel, 2 New Montgomery Street ☎ 415/512–1111 🚃 5, 6, 7, 8, 9, 21, 31, 38, 42, 45, 71

PLOUGH AND STARS

Without gimmicks, this low-key Irish bar performs it function admirably, providing space to drink and chat, and enjoy Irish music.
✚ F6 ✉ 116 Clement Street ☎ 415/751–1122 🚃 2

RED ROOM

Well-dressed martini-sipping revelers descend on this Nob Hill bar whose decor stays true to its name.
✚ K5 ✉ 827 Sutter Street ☎ 415/346–7666 🚃 2, 3, 4, 27, 76

SAN FRANCISCO BREWING COMPANY

Serves a selection of excellent own-brew beers from a 1907 bar. Live music several nights.
✚ K4 ✉ 155 Columbus Avenue ☎ 415/434–3344 🚃 15, 41

STARLIGHT ROOM

Cozy, stylish spot for a rooftop-level drink and a glide around the dance floor to the smooth sounds of the Starlight Orchestra.
✚ K5 ✉ Sir Francis Drake Hotel, 450 Powell Street ☎ 415/395–8595 🚃 2, 3, 4, 76

TONGA ROOM

Full of kirsch, rum drinks and periodic tropical rainstorms, visit this Nob Hill bar to put you in the right mood.
✚ K5 ✉ Fairmont Hotel, 950 Mason Street ☎ 415/772–5278 🚃 1; Powell–Hyde cable car

TORONADO

The various alternative lifestyles that are part and parcel of the Haight-Ashbury neighborhood can be observed at this lively haunt.
✚ H7 ✉ 547 Haight Street ☎ 415/863–2276 🚃 6, 7, 66, 71

LIQUOR LAWS

Bars can legally be open at any time between 6am and 2am, though most choose to open their doors around 11am and close them around midnight (later on Fridays and Saturdays). Provided they are licensed, restaurants can serve liquor throughout their hours of business except between 2am and 6am. To buy or consume liquor legally, customers must be age 21 or older. In a bar, nightclub or restaurant, youthful-looking patrons may well be asked to show proof of their age. Most supermarkets, department stores and dedicated liquor stores sell spirits, wine and beer during regular store hours, though legally they can do so from 6am to 2am.

Cafés

INSIDE CAFÉS

San Francisco is renowned for its proliferation of loosely European-style cafés, found in every neighborhood, and there is no better place to check the pulse of the city. Along with quality coffee and a selection of wholesome snacks, cafés typically provide newspapers (and sometimes books) for their customers; some are noted for their pickup chess games, others for their ambient music or computer with access to the Internet. Uninteresting cafés quickly go out of business.

BUENA VISTA CAFÉ
Good, inexpensive food in a pricey area; known for its punch-packing Irish coffee.
✛ J3 ✉ 2765 Hyde Street ☎ 415/474–5044 ▣ 32

CAFÉ FLORE
The affectionate nicknames applied to this energetic spot— such as Café Haircut and Café Bore—reflect its popularity among a mostly gay clientele.
✛ H8 ✉ 2298 Market Street ☎ 415/621–8579 ▣ 8, 37; F, J, K, L, M, N

CAFFÈ GRECO
A prime place to imbibe the North Beach atmosphere with the aid of an invigorating cappuccino or espresso.
✛ K4 ✉ 423 Columbus Avenue ☎ 415/397–6261 ▣ 15, 30, 41

CAFFÈ ROMA
Sip one of the dozen coffee blends at a marble table.
✛ K4 ✉ 526 Columbus Avenue ☎ 415/296–7942 ▣ 15, 30, 41, 45

CAFFÈ TRIESTE
Since it opened in the 1950s, Trieste has been the quintessential North Beach café, drawing writers, poets, artists and anyone seeking a flavorful cup of coffee and tempting cakes.
✛ K4 ✉ 601 Vallejo Street ☎ 415/982–2605 ▣ 15, 41

ENRICO'S
A long-serving North Beach café that make a visit to its patio tables worthwhile; the often rude service has become, for some, part of the allure.
✛ K4 ✉ 504 Broadway ☎ 415/982–6223 ▣ 12, 15, 41

IL CAFFE EMPORIO RULLI
Facing Union Square and perfect for people watching while munching a pastry and lingering over a coffee.
✛ K5 ✉ Stockton Street Pavillion, Union Square ☎ 415/433–1122 ▣ 2, 3, 4, 30, 76

TARTINE BAKERY
Serves gourmet coffee and selected wines by the glass but the star attractions are the pastries, buns and sandwiches served in a range of inventive, mouthwatering guises.
✛ J8 ✉ 600 Guerrero Street ☎ 415/487–2600 ▣ 33

TOSCA CAFÉ
Opened in 1919 and allegedly serving the first espresso in California, Tosca has opera reverberating from its jukebox and numerous celebrity regulars like Nicolas Cage and Uncle Francis Ford Coppola.
✛ K4 ✉ 242 Columbus Avenue ☎ 415/986–9651 ▣ 15, 41

VESUVIO
A legendary haunt of the original Beats, Vesuvio is still the scene of earnest debate and philosophical conversations.
✛ K4 ✉ 255 Columbus Avenue ☎ 415/362–3370 ▣ 15, 41, 83

Other Ideas

A CLEAN WELL-LIGHTED PLACE FOR BOOKS

An impressive assortment of authors, local and national, show up at this bookstore for signings, readings, and talks.

✚ J6 ✉ 601 Van Ness Avenue ☎ 415/441–6670 🚌 42, 47, 49

AMC KABUKI 8

This eight-screen modern movie complex in the heart of Japantown is the likeliest spot to find the latest Hollywood movies.

✚ H5 ✉ 1881 Post Street, between Buchanan and Webster streets ☎ 415/922–4AMC 🚌 2, 3, 4, 38

CASTRO THEATRE

A 1920s' movie palace, complete with Wurlitzer organ, which makes an atmospheric setting for a daily diet of cult, foreign and revival movies.

✚ H8 ✉ 429 Castro Street ☎ 415/621–6120 🚌 24; K, L, M

CLAY

The city's oldest continuously running cinema, in business since 1912, and a favorite with San Franciscan movie buffs as the main showcase for first-run foreign movies.

✚ H5 ✉ 2261 Fillmore Street ☎ 415/267–4893 🚌 3, 22

COBB'S

Nationally known names top the bill at this 200-seat comedy club every night except Monday "open mic" nights. Reserve in advance for

leading draws.

✚ K3 ✉ 915 Columbus Avenue ☎ 415/928–4320 🚌 15, 30, 41

THE MECHANICS' INSTITUTE

Monthly exhibitions, usually focusing on aspects of San Francisco history, can be enjoyed on weekly guided tours that also highlight the architecture of this 1909 beaux-arts building.

✚ L5 ✉ 57 Post Street ☎ 415/393–0100 🕐 Wed noon 🚌 2, 3, 4, 76

PLAY CHESS

San Francisco holds possibly the oldest chess club in the US, based at the Mechanics' Institute (▶ above). All-comers from beginners to masters are at the Tuesday night marathon tournament, and a two-hour class for kids is held Wednesday afternoons.

☎ 415/421–2258

PRESIDIO BOWLING CENTER

In the stunning Presidio, this 12-lane bowling alley draws a twenty-something crowd from the nearby Marina district.

✚ F4 ✉ Corner of Moraga Avenue and Montgomery Street, the Presidio ☎ 415/561–2695 🕐 Mon–Fri 9am–10pm, Sat–Sun 9am–11pm 🚌 29, 43

PUNCH LINE

Long-running venue for both aspiring and nationally known comedians, with a good record of giving future stars their early break.

✚ L4 ✉ 444 Battery Street ☎ 415/397–7573 🚌 41, 42

SPECTATOR SPORTS

The San Francisco Giants baseball team play at Pacific Bell Park, also known locally as the "Miracle on Third Street," a 40,000-seat stadium opened in April 2000 in a scenic bayside location. Eight miles (13km) south of the city, the Giants previous home, 3Com Park (formerly Candlestick Park) is still a football venue for the San Francisco 49ers. For both sports, a very limited number of tickets are available on match days but most are sold in advance through Ticketmaster (☎ 415/421–TIXS).

STERN GROVE CONCERTS

On Sunday afternoons from June to August, a eucalyptus-shrouded natural amphitheater at Stern Grove offers free concerts and performances ranging from classical music and opera to jazz and modern dance.

✚ Off map at D10 ✉ Sloat Boulevard at 19th Avenue ☎ 415/252–6252 🚌 28

Luxury Hotels

PRICES

You may expect to pay the following prices per night, based (except for hostels) on two people sharing, and excluding taxes:

Luxury	over $200
Mid-range	up to $200
Budget	up to $120
Hostels	$19–23
	(per person)

HOTEL TELEPHONE NUMBERS

Many hotels and some bed-and-breakfast inns can be telephoned using toll-free numbers (prefixed 800, 888, 877 or 866). Remember that these numbers can usually be dialed from anywhere in the United States or Canada, although there is sometimes a different toll-free number for calls made within California (and a few may be available in California only).

ARGENT HOTEL

A taste of modern elegance in the heart of downtown. The 667 chic rooms all offer superb views of the city.
➕ L5 ✉ 50 3rd Street
☎ 415/974–6400 or 888/238–0302; fax 415/ 543–8268; www.argenthotel.com 🖥 15, 30

CAMPTON PLACE

Well placed close to Union Square, with 117 stylish rooms and attentive staff.
➕ K5 ✉ 340 Stockton Street
☎ 800/1010–1111 or 415/781–5555; www.camptonplace.com 🖥 30, 45

FAIRMONT HOTEL AND TOWER

Famous Nob Hill land-mark hotel with 805 sumptuous tower rooms affording lovely views.
➕ K5 ✉ 950 Mason Street
☎ 800/257–7544 or 415/772– 5000; fax 415/772–5013; www.fairmont.com 🖥 1; Powell–Hyde cable car

INN AT THE OPERA

Quiet and elegant, and a favorite of thespians and opera stars for its proximity to the performing-arts halls of Civic Center. 48 rooms.
➕ J6 ✉ 333 Fulton Street
☎ 800/590–0157 or 415/863–8400; fax 415/861–0821; www.innattheopera.com 🖥 5, 21

MANDARIN ORIENTAL

In the heart of the Financial District with 158 large, opulently furnished rooms; some rooms have city views.
➕ L5 ✉ 222 Sansome Street
☎ 800/622–0404 or 415/276–9888; fax 415/433–0289; www.mandarin-oriental.com
🖥 42

RADISSON MIYAKO

Fusing the ideas of East and West, some of the 229 rooms at this Japantown property are designed in Japanese style with tatami mats and futons.
➕ H5 ✉ 1625 Post Street
☎ 800/333–3333 or 415/922–3200; fax 415/921–0417; www.miyakohotel.com 🖥 2, 3, 4

THE PALACE

The city's first luxury hotel, located downtown. Appropriate for royalty, heads of state and any-one with a taste for the finer things. 550 rooms.
➕ L5 ✉ 2 New Montgomery Street ☎ 800/325–3589 or 415/512–1111; fax 415/243–8062; www.sfpalace.com
🚊 Montgomery Street 🖥 5, 6, 7, 8, 9, 21, 31, 38, 42, 45, 71

WESTIN ST. FRANCIS

A San Franciscan landmark since 1904 and resoundingly aristocratic. 1,192 rooms.
➕ K5 ✉ 335 Powell Street at Union Square ☎ 888/625–5144 or 415/397–7000; fax 415/774–0124 🖥 2, 3, 4, 6, 38, 71; Powell–Hyde or Powell–Mason cable car

WHITE SWAN INN

Breakfast buffet and complimentary evening wine adds to the already rich atmosphere of this Nob Hill 26-room, antique-decorated inn.
➕ K5 ✉ 845 Bush Street
☎ 800/999–9570 or 415/775–1755; fax 415/775–5717; www.jdvhospitality.com/hotels/hotel/16 🖥 2, 3, 4, 76

Mid-Range Hotels

ALAMO SQUARE INN
Offers a choice of antiques-filled or high-tech accommodations in two adjoining Victorians in the Western Addition. Breakfast and evening wine included. 14 rooms.
➕ H6 ✉ 719 Scott Street
☎ 866/515–0123 or 415/315–0123; fax 415/315–0108; www.alamoinn.com 📟 21

ARCHBISHOP'S MANSION
Transformed from a genuine 1904 arch-bishop's Alamo Square residence to an inn with 15 antiques-filled rooms. Breakfast included.
➕ H6 ✉ 1000 Fulton Street
☎ 800/543–5820 (in California) or 415/563–7872; fax 415/885–3193 📟 5, 21

BIJOU
San Francisco-set movies provide the cue for 65 themed rooms. Close to Union Square. Breakfast included.
➕ K5 ✉ 111 Mason Street
☎ 800/771–1022 or 415/771–1200 📟 38

CANTERBURY HOTEL
A welcoming downtown hotel with an English manor house theme; decorated with 1930s murals of the *Canterbury Tales*. 255 rooms.
➕ K5 ✉ 750 Sutter Street
☎ 415/474–6464 or 800/227–4788; fax 415/474–0831
📟 2, 3, 4, 76

DRISCO HOTEL
Breakfast and evening wine are included in the cost of this 100-year-old, 48-room hotel in well-heeled Pacific Heights.
➕ G5 ✉ 2901 Pacific Heights
☎ 800/634–7277 or 415/346–2880; fax 415/567–5537; www.jdvhospitality.com/hotels/hotel/6 📟 3, 24

MONACO HOTEL
Affordable luxury, offering 201 well-appointed rooms within an easy walk of Union Square. A pet friendly hotel where they will even provide a goldfish in your room for company.
➕ K5 ✉ 501 Geary Street
☎ 866/622–5284; fax 415/292–0111; www.monaco-sf.com
📟 38

RENOIR HOTEL
A likeable flatiron-shaped Civic Center landmark that houses 135 simple but comfortable rooms. Market Street side can be noisy.
➕ K6 ✉ 45 McAllister Street
☎ 415/626–5200 or 800/576–3388; fax 415/626–0916; www.renoirhotel.com 📟 Any Market Street bus

STANYAN PARK HOTEL
Small, friendly hotel next to Golden Gate Park. Breakfast included. 36 rooms.
➕ F7 ✉ 750 Stanyan Street
☎ 415/751–1000; fax 415/668–5454; www.stanyanpark.com
📟 6, 7, 33, 43, 66, 71

TRITON
Union Square hotel tailor-made for trend-conscious travelers with bold and arty designs throughout. 140 rooms.
➕ K5 ✉ 342 Grant Avenue
☎ 800/800–1299 or 415/394–0500; fax 415/394–0555; www.hoteltriton.com 📟 2, 3, 4, 76

BOOKINGS
Reservations should be made as early as possible, either by phone, fax or mail. A deposit (usually by credit card) equivalent to the nightly rate will ensure your room is held at least until 6pm; if you are arriving later, inform the hotel. Credit card is the usual payment method; traveler's checks or cash can be used but payment will then be expected in advance. The total charge will include the city's 14 percent accommodations tax.

Budget Accommodations

BED-AND-BREAKFAST

San Francisco's bed-and-breakfast inns, which are typically converted Victorian homes sumptuously furnished and stuffed with antiques, offer a friendly alternative to hotels. Bed-and-breakfast owners will often attend to guests personally, serving them a healthy home-cooked breakfast, and will readily pass on their knowledge of the city. Reflecting the fact that both the individual properties and the rooms within them can vary greatly, bed-and-breakfast establishments spanning all price categories are found all over the city. Advance reservation is always recommended. Bed-and-breakfast accommodations can be arranged through:

**Bed & Breakfast
San Francisco**
✉ P.O. Box 420009, San Francisco, CA 94142
☎ 415/889-0060 or 800/452-8249
website: www.bbsf.com

California Association of Bed and Breakfast Inns
✉ 2715 Portal Street, Soquel, CA 95037 ☎ 831/462-9191; www.cabbie.com

ADELAIDE HOTEL & HOSTEL

A lovely pension with 18 bright, clean rooms, situated in the Financial District.
✚ K5 ✉ 5 Isadora Duncan Court (off Taylor Street, between Geary and Post streets)
☎ 877/359-1915 or 415/359-1915; fax 415/359-1940; www.adelaidehostel.com ▣ 2, 3, 4, 38, 76

24 HENRY

A five-room guest house in the Castro district, run by and chiefly aimed at gay men. Breakfast included.
✚ H7 ✉ 24 Henry Street
☎ 800/900-5686 or 415/864-5686; fax 415/864-0406; www.24henry.com ▣ 24, 37

HOSTELLING INTERNATIONAL SAN FRANCISCO FORT MASON

Over 600 hostel beds, mostly in small dorms with some private rooms, are available at the three sites of Hostelling International, at City Center, Downtown and Fort Mason. All three offer luggage storage, self-catering kitchens, internet access, and all are easily reached by bus.
City Center ✚ J5/6 ✉ 685 Ellis Street ☎ 415/474-5721; fax 415/776-0775 ▣ 27
Downtown ✚ K5 ✉ 312 Mason Street ☎ 415/788-5604; fax 415/788-3203 ▣ 38
Fort Mason ✚ H3 ✉ Building 240, Fort Mason ☎ 415/771-7277; fax 415/771-1468 ▣ 28, 42, 49

HOTEL DES ARTS

Decorated by local artists whose work also features in the gallery; the least costly of the 51 rooms have wash basins and shared bathrooms, while others have private facilities. Continental breakfast included.
✚ K5 ✉ 447 Bush Street
☎ 800/956-4322 or 415/956-3232; fax 415/956-0399 ▣ 2, 3, 4, 76

MARINA MOTEL

Plain and simple motel on the north edge of Pacific Heights, with a choice of regular and kitchen-equipped rooms.
✚ G4 ✉ 2576 Lombard Street ☎ 800/346-6118 or 415/921-9406; fax 415/931-0364; www.marinamotel.com ▣ 28, 43, 76

TOWN HOUSE MOTEL

Simply furnished, well kept and in a convenient Marina location. Continental breakfast included.
✚ H4 ✉ 1650 Lombard Street ☎ 800/255-1516 or 415/885-5163; fax 415/771-9889; www.sftownhousemotel.com ▣ 76

VILLAGE HOUSE

Choice of five tastefully-themed and decorated rooms, from Asian to art deco, in the Castro. The establishment includes internet access and the chance to play the parlors piano.
✚ H8 ✉ 4080 18th Street
☎ 800/900-5686 or 415/864-0994; fax 415/864-0406; www.24henry.com ▣ 33

SAN FRANCISCO's
travel facts

29 SUNSET
To 3rd St/Paul
Daily Approx 7AM-6:30PM

INFORMATION:
DIAL 673-MUNI

ESSENTIAL FACTS

Electricity
- The supply is 100 volts, 60 cycles AC current.
- US appliances use two-prong plugs. European appliances require an adapter.

Etiquette
- Be aware of the anti-smoking feeling that prevails in San Francisco. Smoking is illegal in bars, restaurants and nightclubs throughout California.
- Tip at least 15 percent in a restaurant; 15–20 percent of a taxi fare; $1 per bag to a porter.

Lavatories
- Public buildings are obliged to provide lavatories, which are almost always well maintained, as are those in hotel lobbies, restaurants and most bars.

Money matters
- Nearly all banks have Automatic Teller Machines (ATMs).
- Credit cards are widely accepted.
- An 8.5 percent sales tax is added to marked retail prices.
- Funds can be wired via: American Express MoneyGram ☎ 800/926–9400 for US and Canada locations; Western Union ☎ 800/325–6000 for agent locations (or to send using MasterCard or Visa)

Opening hours
- Stores: Mon–Sat 9 or 10–5 or 6. Department stores, shopping centers and stores aimed at tourists keep longer hours and are also open on Sundays.
- Banks: Mon–Fri 9–4, 5 or 6; some branches open Saturdays.
- Post office: usually Mon–Fri 9–5.30, with limited hours on Saturday.

Places of worship
- Hotel receptions can advise and the phone book carries a comprehensive list.

Public holidays
- Jan 1: New Year's Day
- Third Mon in Jan: Martin Luther King Day
- Third Mon in Feb: President's Day
- Mar 31: Cesar Chavez Day
- Last Mon in May: Memorial Day
- Jul 4: Independence Day
- First Mon in Sep: Labor Day
- Second Mon in Oct: Columbus Day
- Nov 11: Veterans' Day
- Fourth Thu in Nov: Thanksgiving Day
- Dec 25: Christmas Day

Visitor information
- San Francisco Convention & Visitor Bureau ⊠ 900 Market Street, Hallidie Plaza, CA ☎ 415/391–2000; www. sfvisitor.org. Their 80-page *San Francisco Book* (free in the US) has details of theaters, exhibits, sports and other events.
- The Redwood Empire Tourist Center ⊠ c/o The California Welcome Center, Pier 39, Suite P214B, San Francisco, CA 94133 ☎ 415/956–3493 covers San Francisco, the Wine Country, the redwood groves and northwestern California. At no cost they will mail *The Redwood Adventures Guide* that you can also get at their office.
- Convention and Visitors Bureaus in San Francisco Bay Area cities: Berkeley ⊠ 2015 Center Street, Berkeley, CA 94704 ☎ 510/549–7040 Oakland ⊠ 463 11th Street, Oakland CA 94607 ☎ 510/839–9000 San Jose ⊠ 408 Almaden Boulevard, San Jose, CA 95110 ☎ 800/726–5673

Santa Clara ✉ 1850 Warburton Avenue, Santa Clara, CA 95054 ☎ 800/272–6822

- For a free travel package including the *California Visitors Guide* and state map ☎ 800/862–2543
- Public library ✉ 100 Larkin Street (also at Grove Street) ☎ 415/557–4400

PUBLIC TRANSPORTATION

BART

- Fares range from $1.25 to $6.90 according to distance traveled. Tickets can be bought from machines at BART stations.
- Operating times: Mon–Fri 4am–midnight, Sat 6am–midnight, Sun 8am–midnight.
- All BART stations display maps of the BART system. Information ☎ 415/989–2278

Buses

- Bus routes are shown in the phone book and at most bus stops. Maps and timetables are available from City Hall and, in a style more accessible for visitors (and including BART routes), from the Visitor Center Hallidie Plaza.

Taxis

- Taxis can be hailed in the street or from taxi stands at major hotels and at transport terminals.
- During rush hours (7–9am and 4–6pm) and rain, it is hard to find a free taxi cruising the streets. Average taxi fares are $2.85 for pick up and $2.40 for each mile.
- Hotel receptionists can order a taxi for you on request, or you can phone one of the following firms: De Soto ☎ 415/970–1300 Fog City ☎ 415/285–3800 Veteran's ☎ 415/552–1313 Yellow ☎ 415/626–2345
- For further information on public transportation ➤ 7.

DRIVING

Car rental

- All international car-rental companies have desks at San Francisco airport as well as offices in the city.
- Avis: SFO ☎ 800/230–4898
- Alamo: SFO ☎ 800/462–5266
- Budget Rent-a-Car: SFO ☎ 800/527–0700
- Dollar: SFO ☎ 800/800–4000
- Dubbelju (motorcycles) ☎ 415/495–2774
- Hertz: SFO ☎ 800/654–3131

Fining

- On-the-spot fines can be imposed for speeding: between $80 and $140 depending on the amout over the limit. Over 25mph (40kph), you may have to go to court.

Headlights

- Low-beam headlights must be used one half hour after sunset to one half hour before sunrise or when conditions (particularly in fog) reduce visibility to less than 1,000ft (305m).

Parking

- Parking restrictions are enforced with vigor. San Francisco has many off-street and multistory parking lots in addition to meters which take quarters only.
- When parking on the city's steep hills, you are required by law to turn downhill facing vehicle's front wheels into the curb and uphill facing vehicles should have their wheels turned to the street.

Seatbelts

- Seatbelts are compulsory for all passengers in front and rear seats. Child restraints are mandatory for under 4-year olds weighing up to 40 lbs (88kg).

Speed limits

- Unless posted higher, the limit is 25mph (40kph) in school zones, business and residential areas.
- Maximum speed on freeways is 65mph (105kph), 70mph (113kph) where specifically posted, except on downtown freeways where it is 55mph (89kph), and on construction zones.
- San Francisco's grid of streets includes steep hills and a convoluted one-way system. Pedestrians and cable cars always have right of way. There is a toll for drivers coming south across the Golden Gate Bridge, and west across the Bay Bridge.
- If you belong to a motoring organization, check its links with the AAA California State Automobile Association, who offer free maps to members ✉ 150 Van Ness Avenue ☎ 415/565–2141

Turns

- Right turns on red are permitted after a stop except where posted.
- Left turns are always permitted (unless posted otherwise) from a one-way to another one-way lane, and from a two-way street to a left one-way or two-way street.
- Except where otherwise posted, U-turns are permitted where visibility is unobstructed for 200 feet (61m) in each direction. U-turns in business districts are only permitted at intersections or two-way left turn lanes.

MEDIA & COMMUNICATIONS

Newspapers & magazines

- San Francisco has two daily newspapers, the *San Francisco Chronicle* and the *San Francisco Examiner*, and two free weekly papers, *SF Weekly* and *San Francisco Bay Guardian* (➤ 5).
- Free tourist-aimed magazines are found in hotel lobbies; their discount coupons can save money on sightseeing and food.

Post services

- Stamps are available from post offices and also at some hotel receptions, vending machines and ATMs.
- Find the nearest post office by looking in the phone book or asking at your hotel.

Telephones

- Public telephones are found in the street, hotel lobbies, restaurants and most public buildings.
- Many businesses have toll-free numbers, prefixed 800, 866, 877 or 888, allowing the public to phone them for free. First dial "1."
- Most US phones use touch-tone dialing, each button issues a different electronic tone as it is pressed, enabling the caller to access extensions directly, following the instructions given by a recorded voice.
- The area code for San Francisco is 415, which should not be dialed if calling from another 415 number. The code for Berkeley and Oakland is 510.
- To call the operator dial "0."

Television & radio

- Linked to national networks, the main San Francisco TV channels are 2, KTVU (FOX); 4, KRON (NBC); 5, KPIX (CBS); 7, KGO (ABC); and the public-run 9, KQED (PBS). These give the usual range of programs plus local and national news.
- San Francisco has some 80 radio

stations. Generally, the best talk and news shows are on the AM waveband, the best music on FM stations.

EMERGENCIES

Embassies & consulates
- Germany ⊠ 1960 Jackson Street
  ☎ 415/775–1061
- Ireland ⊠ 100 Pine Street
  ☎ 415/392–4214
- Italy ⊠ 2590 Webster Street
  ☎ 415/931–4924
- Japan ⊠ 50 Fremont Street
  ☎ 415/777–3533
- Mexico ⊠ 532 Folsom Street
  ☎ 415/354–1700
- Spain ⊠ 1405 Sutter Street
  ☎ 415/922–2995
- UK ⊠ 1 Sansome Street, Suite 850
  ☎ 415/671–1300

Emergency phone numbers
- Fire, police or ambulance ☎ 911
- Rape Crisis Hotline ☎ 415/647–7273
- Victims of Crime Resource Center
  ☎ 800/842–8467

Lost property
- San Francisco International Airport ☎ 650/821–7014
- Amtrak station in Oakland ☎ 510/238–4320
- MUNI buses or cable cars ☎ 415/923–6168

Medical treatment
- Doctor referral: San Francisco Medical Society ☎ 415/561–0850
- Dentist: San Francisco Dental Society ☎ 415/928–7337
- City hospitals with 24-hour emergency rooms: San Francisco General ⊠ 1001 Potrero Avenue ☎ 415/206–8000; Davies Medical Center ⊠ Castro Street (at Duboce Street) ☎ 415/565–6000
- Medicines: 24-hour pharmacy

Walgreens offers a service at:
⊠ 3201 Divisadero Street ☎ 415/931–6417;
⊠ 498 Castro Street ☎ 415/861–3136
- It is strongly recommended to take out comprehensive medical insurance before traveling.

Medicines
- Pharmacies are plentiful and can be found in the *Yellow Pages* listed under "Drugstores."
- Visitors from Europe will find many familiar medicines are sold under unfamiliar names. Note that some medication bought over the counter at home might be prescription only in the US and may be confiscated at customs. Bring a doctor's certificate for essential medication.

Sensible precautions
- San Francisco is one of the country's safest cities and lone travelers, especially women, are not unusual. Unwelcome attention is not unknown, and areas such as the Tenderloin, parts of the Mission, Oakland, SoMa, the Haight, Golden Gate Park, Western Addition and the outskirts of the city, may seem (and may be) threatening after dark.
- Do not carry easily snatched bags and cameras, or stuff your wallet into your back pocket. Always keep your belongings within sight and within reach.
- Keep valuables in the hotel's safe and never carry more cash than you need.
- If you plan to make an insurance claim, report any item stolen to the nearest police precinct as soon as possible. It is unlikely that any stolen goods will be recovered, but the police will fill out the forms that your insurance company will need.

93

Index

CityPack
San Francisco *Top 25*

ABOUT THE AUTHOR

Mick Sinclair is a frequent visitor to San Francisco and has also written guides to California, Chicago, Miami, New York and Scandinavia. His magazine and newspaper features on travel, music, books, film and other aspects of contemporary culture have appeared in newspapers and magazines throughout the world. Much of his journalism can be read online at http://micksinclair.com

AUTHOR AND EDITION REVISER Mick Sinclair **CONTRIBUTIONS TO "WHERE TO"** Julie Jares
MANAGING EDITORS Apostrophe S Limited **COVER DESIGN** Tigist Getachew, Fabrizio La Rocca

A CIP catalogue record for this book is available from the British Library.

ISBN-10: 0-7495-4749-9
ISBN-13: 978-0-7495-4749-3

Published by AA Publishing (a trading name of Automobile Association Developments Limited, whose registered office is at Fanum House, Basing View, Basingstoke, Hampshire RG21 4EA. Registered number 1878835).

© AUTOMOBILE ASSOCIATION DEVELOPMENTS LIMITED 1996, 1999, 2002, 2003, 2006
First published 1996. Reprinted 1996. Second edition 1998. Reprinted Mar 1999. Third edition 1999. Fourth edition 2002. Fifth edition 2003. Reprinted Jun 2004. Reprinted Mar 2005.
Sixth edition 2006.

Colour separation by Keenes, Andover
Printed and bound in Hong Kong by Hang Tai D&P Limited

ACKNOWLEDGEMENTS
The Automobile Association would like to thank the following photographers, picture libraries and associations for their assistance in the preparation of this book: BRIDGEMAN ART LIBRARY Rock concert poster for the Doors and others at the Avalon Ballroom San Francisco, 14 June 1967 by Victor Moscoso (20th century) Private Collection 17r; CARTOON ART MUSEUM 55; COURTESY OF THE DE YOUNG MUSEUM, SAN FRANCISCO 29; GETTY IMAGES 9b, 10/11, 11ct, 11cb, 14/15; ROBERT HARDING PICTURE LIBRARY 12, 19l